Vicki Pitman, a nativ[e ...] qualified herbalist, na[turopath and] Ayurvedic practitioner. She is a m[emb]er of the American Herbalists Guild, the Unified Register of Herbal Practitioners and the International Federation of Aromatherapists. Vicki combines clinical work near her home in Somerset, England, with teaching, writing and research into herbal and other holistic medicine disciplines. She has completed an MPhil in Complementary Health Studies (Exeter University) on holism in ancient Greek and Indian medicine.

A note on safety and herb/drug interaction

Evidence shows that herbs are generally safe and act with fewer side effects and dangers than conventional drugs. There may be, rarely, an idiosyncratic reaction to a herb – one that is unexpected, unexplained and individual to a particular person, a 'one-off' – as indeed there can be to even a simple food. As more people are using herbs while also taking conventional drug therapy from their medical practitioner the possibility, largely theoretical, exists that there are certain circumstances in which a herb's properties or the way the body processes a herb can affect the way it processes the drug and/or the drug's effect. This is also true of certain foods – for example, grapefruit and coffee. Interactions are uncommon compared with those arising from multi-drug ingestion and usually less serious. To date herbs known to have this effect include: St. John's Wort (*Hypericum perforatum*), Ephedra (*Ephedra sinica*), Valerian (*Valerian officinalis*), Kava (*Piper methysticum*), Licorice (*Licorice glycyrrhiza*), Ginkgo (*Gingko biloba*), Oak bark (*Quercus robar*), Sarsaparilla (*Smilax spp.*), and Chasteberry (*Vitex agnus castus*).

This does not mean you cannot take herbs and drug medications at the same time, but that if you do, just as you would inform your herbalist if you were taking drugs, you need to inform your doctor fully so that the appropriate monitoring and adjustments can be made. It is especially important to do this if you will be undergoing an operation.

'New Perspectives' series

'New Perspectives' provide attractive and accessible introductions to a comprehensive range of mind, body, and spirit topics. Beautifully designed and illustrated, these practical books are written by experts in each subject.

Books in the series:

Alexander Technique, Richard Brennan
Aromatherapy, Christine Wildwood
Crystal Therapy, Stephanie and Tim Harrison
Dreams, David Fontana
Flower Remedies, Christine Wildwood
Herbal Remedies, Vicki Pitman
Homeopathy, Peter Adams
Nutritional Therapy, Jeannette Ewin

New Perspectives

HERBAL REMEDIES

An Introductory Guide to Herbs for Health and Well-Being

VICKI PITMAN M.PHIL, A.H.G, U.R.H.P, IFPA,ENI

vega

First Published by Element Books Ltd, 2000
© Vega 2002
Text © Vicki Pitman 2000

All rights reserved. No part of this book may be reproduced, stored
in a retrieval system or transmitted in any form or by any means,
electronic, mechanical, photocopying, recording or otherwise,
without the prior permission in writing of the copyright owners.

ISBN 1-84333-074-1

A catalogue record for this book is available
from the British Library

Published in 2002 by
Vega
64 Brewery Road
London, N7 9NT

A member of **Chrysalis** Books plc

Visit our website at www.chrysalisbooks.co.uk

Printed in Great Britain
by CPD, Wales

Contents

Introduction 8

1 The History of Herbal Medicine 11

2 How Herbs Heal 20

3 Herbal Energy and Constitutional Types 27

4 The Therapeutic Actions of Herbs 36

5 Hands-on Herbs 47

6 Materia Medica 62

7 Remedies for Common Ailments 100

Useful Addresses 120

Further Reading 122

Sources of Herbal Supplies 123

Glossary 124

Index 126

Acknowledgements

I would like to thank and give my appreciation to the outstanding teachers who have guided and inspired me in my herbal studies: Farida Sharan, Michael and Lesley Tierra, Dr Vasant Lad.

I extend thanks to my herbalist and Ayurvedic colleague Anthony Deavin for his valuable help; to my students and clients in Somerset who are also my teachers; and to the technical staff at Yeovil College for their assistance.

I am particularly grateful to my husband and daughters for their patience and co-operation; to my brothers and sisters for their support; and to my mother, who instilled in me a love of the wild.

NOTE FROM THE PUBLISHER
Any information given in any book in the New Perspectives series is not intended to be taken as a replacement for medical advice. Any person with a condition requiring medical attention should consult a qualified medical practitioner or suitable therapist.

Foreword

There is a beautiful tale told by the Cherokee of how the Green People came to the aid of human beings.

'In the beginning of this world, all creatures could speak a common language, and respected and understood one another, taking only what they needed to live. Gradually, however, humans began to abuse their place in the Great Life: they took more than they needed, lacked respect for fellow creatures, trampled on others carelessly. The other animals held councils to try to decide how to solve the problem of man, but could think of no plan that would work. Finally, the insects thought up the idea of giving diseases to humans to kill them off, and diseases began to appear among humans, but although many died, many survived. The insects then went to the Green People, the plants, for help in totally destroying arrogant humanity. After four days of deliberation, Grandfather Ginseng, the chief of the Green People, replied, "We have heard your words and there is much truth in them. People have hurt and abused us as much or more than they have you. But we are all part of the same Great Life. So we have decided that if people come to us in a good way, a sacred way, we will help them by giving them the cure for every disease that you, the insects, have made."'

Based on a story related by David Winston, herbalist, Cherokee nation, in *American Herbalism*, Essays by Members of the American Herbalists Guild.

INTRODUCTION

Herbal medicine is humankind's oldest medicine and is also the subject of much current scientific interest. It is as near to us as the geranium on the windowsill, the thyme in the garden and the grass in the meadow. For the minor upsets, ailments and accidents of daily life, herbs are not only effective medicine, they also help maintain the body's overall energy and strength, connect us to our wider environment, enhance our self-awareness and help develop our intuitive nature.

How Does Herbal Medicine Work?

Herbal medicine makes use of the whole plant in treatments for the whole person. Like other natural medicine therapies, it views humans as part of nature and therefore observes and works with nature's gifts in the management of disease.

LEFT MANY HERBS ARE EXTREMELY EASY TO GROW AND CAN BE KEPT IN SMALL POTS ON THE WINDOWSILL READY FOR INSTANT MEDICINAL USE.

LEFT HERBAL MEDICINE WORKS ON THE WHOLE PERSON – THEIR MENTAL, EMOTIONAL AND PHYSICAL STATES – TO RESTORE BALANCE AND WELL-BEING.

It is believed that within all of nature there exists a common life principle – the vital or life force. It is called *ch'i* in Chinese, *prana* in Indian and *rooh* in Islamic-Tibb traditional medicine. The ancient Greeks knew it as *pneuma*. The free flow and expression of this life force, encompassing the mental, emotional and physical state of the person, constitutes health. Disease is said to result when this flow is obstructed or impaired, causing imbalances in the body, which are experienced as the symptoms of illness.

Plant energy can nourish and strengthen the whole body at the same time as it attends to particular symptoms. Treatment with herbs is designed to resolve imbalances and restore the healthy function of the whole system, as well as specific organs. Herbs can treat the underlying, sometimes subtle, causes of disease, as well as its manifestations as pain, inflammation or fatigue, and help to foster the positive natural healing force of the body.

Herbal medicine is a form of energetic medicine – it uses the qualities and energy of herbs to influence and harmonize with the qualities and energy of the individual person, as the same life principle, or vital force, is common to both.

RIGHT THE HEALING PROPERTIES OF A PLANT SUCH AS ECHINACEA WORK ON THE UNDERLYING CAUSES OF A DISEASE, NOT JUST ON THE SYMPTOMS ALONE.

Herbal medicine is not an unscientific medicine. In using it, we are not denying scientific knowledge or choosing superstition over fact. Every year, more and more traditional remedies, once ridiculed by modern orthodox physicians, are being confirmed by scientific research and espoused by medical doctors as their efficacy is proven.

Using the Whole Plant

It is said that herbal medicine uses the whole plant. This does not mean that all parts of the plant are always used, but that the part used – root, bark, leaves, flower or seed – will be taken complete as nature provided it. This contrasts with orthodox medicine, which tries to isolate a single 'active' chemical component to give as medicine. Herbalists, while aware of these individual components of a plant, find that they work best when they stay with their natural molecular companions. This synergy – the combined effect of all the parts working together being greater than the sum of the parts working individually – helps keep herbal medicines free from damaging side-effects. With whole-plant medicine, one component affects one bodily part, while another simultaneously affects a different part. Both moderate each other's influences, balancing each other and creating a more harmonious effect on the body.

THE HISTORY OF HERBAL MEDICINE

CHAPTER ONE

The origins of herbal medicine date from the first human life, for humans have always used plants for food and medicine. The first herbals represent the recording of knowledge built up over millennia of experience and passed down through oral tradition.

In this book, it is only possible to trace the general outlines of the ideas and practices of herbal medicine based on written records. However, it is important to remember that alongside this runs the unwritten knowledge of the non-professional, mainly rural people – gathered, developed and passed from generation to generation – the so-called folk remedies.

RIGHT EARLY HUMANS USED BERRIES FOR BOTH FOOD AND MEDICINAL PURPOSES.

WESTERN HERBAL MEDICINE

THE ANCIENT EGYPTIANS
In ancient Egypt, herbs were used for religious purposes, as cosmetics and for healing. Many plants and their extraction methods are depicted on the walls of tombs, indicating their central role in Egyptian life. Fragments of medical papyri from about 2000 BC give

LEFT JUNIPER WAS ONE OF THE HERBS USED FOR HEALING AND RITUAL IN ANCIENT EGYPT.

instructions and recipes for preparing various herbal medicaments including unguents, poultices and beverages made from herbs such as juniper, licorice, sweet calamus and aloe vera. Herbs were also extensively used in the mummification process.

THE ANCIENT GREEKS

In classical times little, if any, distinction was made between Hippocratic medicine and natural philosophy. Physicians shared the view of the world that held that humans are a microcosm of the universal macrocosm of nature. All things in nature derive from the same source and partake of its vital energy, or *pneuma*. The fundamental elements in nature, Earth, Water, Fire and Air-Ether form in the human body the biological humours of phlegm, blood, yellow bile and black bile. Health comes from a balanced mingling, or *krasis* of the humours, which leads to a state of well-being or *harmonia*. The Hippocratic physicians advocated the use of special diets, fasting, herbs and habits to harmonize the particular balance of humours within each individual.

Two ancient Greeks who also played an important part in the history of herbal medicine were Dioscorides and Galen. Dioscorides, a surgeon in the Roman army, wrote a five-volume *De Materia Medica* in the first century AD, which was subsequently used for centuries by herbalists.

In the second century AD, Galen, a Greek physician in the employment of the Emperor Marcus Aurelius, praised Dioscorides' work and based much of his use of herbs on it. Galen was a physician of considerable experience and wrote numerous treatises on the arts of medicine and on his investigations into anatomy and physiology. Galen also wrote numerous commentaries on the works of his predecessors and contemporaries. Because of his prestige and the survival of many of his writings, Galen was to be the dominant influence on all subsequent medical thought until the Renaissance, some 1,600 years later.

ISLAMIC MEDICINE

Perhaps the most important Arab physician and teacher was Abu Ah al-Husayn Abd Allah Ibn Sina, known in the West as Avicenna. Born in AD 980, Avicenna, who was a court physician in Persia, was a man of learning in many fields besides medicine – including mathematics, astrology and philosophy. He was also an early chemist and perfected several processes such as filtration, sublimation, calcination and distillation – producing the first essential oil of rose. Avicenna wrote many books, the most famous being his *Canon of Medicine*, which greatly influenced the development of medicine and chemistry, not only in the Middle East, but also in Europe and India.

Arabian civilization established the practice of founding public hospitals and dispensaries for the sick. Today Islamic medicine, which is known as Unani-Tibb, continues to be practised throughout the former Islamic empire, from North Africa to the Indian subcontinent and Indonesia.

PRESERVERS OF HERBAL KNOWLEDGE IN THE WEST

Herbal medicine continued to be studied and used in Europe, by monks and nuns and by gifted individuals. The monasteries and convents maintained special gardens for cultivating medicinal plants. Among lay people too, there was usually someone, often a wise woman, who had a knowledge of healing herbs.

In the later Middle Ages and with the Renaissance in the 15th century, an explosion of learning began, stimulated by increased contacts with the Islamic empire through the Crusades. Ancient Latin and Greek texts were rediscovered during this period and the first medical school was started in Salerno, Italy. The superior medical knowledge of the Arabs was eagerly sought, their texts re-translated into Latin and their teachers invited to teach in newly established medical schools.

Paracelsus

In the 16th century, a Swiss named Paracelsus began to question current medical practices, which he believed were corrupt and stagnant. Paracelsus saw physicians creating elaborate concoctions of dozens of exotic herbs and charging enormous fees, when he knew that in most instances simpler ones would have worked as well. For him, too, many exotic herbs were used and herbs in general used improperly because physicians merely practised without question what they had learned from text books and not from their own observations in the field. He came in like a new broom to sweep away the cobwebs.

Paracelsus was also interested in the new science of chemistry and the effect of metals on the human body, having seen new diseases appearing among local mine-workers heavily exposed to metals. He had his own laboratory and spent hours conducting investigations, but he remained equally devoted to simple, local folk remedies, which he readily used. He gave them, however, a new guiding principle: discarding the humoural doctrine, he felt that each plant had a singular and specific action on specific diseases.

THE AGE OF HERBAL EXPLORATION

From the 1400s, the newly consolidated European nation states such as Britain, France and Spain began exploring and colonizing other parts of the world. In the wake of this, an explosion of interest in and collection of medicinal plants began. Herbs of the East were among the most sought after and expensive commodities of trade, not only for use in foods and perfumes but also for medicines.

The traffic was not totally one way. In the US, colonists brought with them their own herbs and, unintentionally, their own weeds as seeds embedded in clothing or among animals. Native Americans

LEFT COLONISTS BROUGHT PLANTAIN FROM EUROPE TO THE UNITED STATES.

were quick to make use of the medicinal ones such as plantain, which they called 'white man's foot'. In China, the discovery of a new variety of ginseng from North America was welcomed and its curative properties so highly valued that a thriving trade began that continues to this day.

In the 16th and 17th centuries, new herbals began to be written, not in Latin for scholars, but in the language of the lay people. One of the most famous of these herbals was Nicholas Culpepper's *Complete Herbal and English Physician*.

PARTING OF THE WAYS

During the next three centuries Western medicine began to diverge from its common path with traditional herb-based systems. Physicians were becoming more and more influenced by the new developments in physics and chemistry. Instead of the universe consisting of elements of Fire, Water, Earth and Air, it was understood in terms of atoms and molecules. The idea of the balance and harmony between things changed to one of physical forces acting on matter in an exclusively material universe. The heart, for example, came to be seen in mechanistic terms as simply a pump, purged of its poetical-spiritual significance for health. The laws of physics and the discoveries of chemists now allowed matter to be manipulated. The individual constituents of herbs were capable of being isolated and

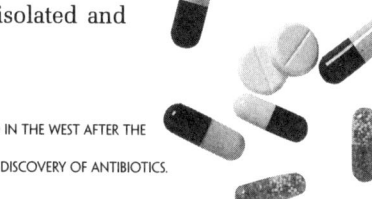

RIGHT HERBAL MEDICINE DECLINED IN THE WEST AFTER THE DISCOVERY OF ANTIBIOTICS.

analysed as single entities, like the simpler compounds of metals. Herbs were gradually discredited in favour of synthetic drugs.

When French chemist Louis Pasteur (1822–1895) perceived bacteria through the microscope, he shifted the whole thrust of medical science firmly away from sustaining health to heroically overcoming disease by the use of drugs to kill germs. The 'magic bullets' of vaccines and drugs did indeed seem to be capable of conquering disease altogether, and the scientists and doctors who delivered them soon became the new gods or priests.

NORTH AMERICA

Meanwhile, herbal medicine, though out of favour with the academic and scientific establishment, was not totally abandoned. The poorer, agricultural and working classes continued to depend on herbal remedies. In the late 18th and early 19th century in the US, Samuel Thompson created a new system of herbal and naturopathic medicine. It was based on the Native American use of herbs and their methods of sweating and purging. His method was to restore the 'vital heat' of the body with warming and stimulating herbs. Although he was hounded by the establishment, who prosecuted him for murder, Thompson's system became very popular. One of his students, Dr Coffin, brought his methods to England in 1838 where, as in the US, they struck a chord with many people.

Another US medical doctor, Wooster Beach, tried to steer medicine back to the use of herbs, and created a system called Eclecticism. He was ostracized by medical colleagues but again his methods became popular because they worked well – they were extremely successful in curing hundreds of cases during cholera epidemics. In both Britain and the US, these 'irregular' herbal systems existed alongside a growing medical science. However, in the early part of the 20th century, a systematic campaign was launched by the American Medical Association to drive out the 'Irregulars' altogether and make their practices illegal, and herbal medicine was again relegated exclusively to the realms of folk medicine.

In the US, one figure in particular stands out in the recent history of herbal medicine – Dr John Christopher, who died in 1983. His work provides a link between the knowledge of the Irregulars and Eclectics, and the present-day return of interest in herbal medicine. During the 1960s and 1970s many young people, having lost faith in allopathic medicine, went to learn from him and others like him. He became the godfather of a new generation of American herbalists.

Concurrently, Native Americans, whose skills have always been a strong but unacknowledged part of US and European botanical medicine since the 17th century, began to share their traditions more openly with the now receptive white Americans.

EUROPE

In Britain, the herbalists' right to practise was protected by a charter from Henry VIII. They formed the Association of Medical Herbalists (now the National Institute of Medical Herbalists), and in 1911 a training school was founded, which continues to this day. In the 1960s, the outstanding herbalist Fred Fletcher-Hyde succeeded in establishing the right of qualified herbalists to practise and prescribe in their own right. This was included in The Medicines Act of 1968.

Natural healers on mainland Europe such as Father Sebastian Kniepp in the 19th century and later Dr Bircher-Brenner and Dr Vogel in the 20th century continued to use herbal remedies successfully. In France, the traditional herbalist Maurice Messegué was justly famous and consulted by all manner of people, including statesmen and celebrities. In Russia and Germany, scientific 'progress' did not lead to such a rift between herbal and allopathic medicine, and investigation of the efficacy of traditional herbs has meant that herbs are well respected in these countries and prescribed by doctors as well as by herbalists.

In the past 20 years there has been a huge renewal of interest in practising herbal medicine as a career. Older colleges have found an increase in applications and newer ones have sprung up to satisfy the demand for training.

Herbal Medicine in Other Cultures

While herbalism has just about managed to survive in Western culture and is growing again, it has never been abandoned by peoples and physicians of other cultures. Chinese medicine, in addition to its now well-known technique of acupuncture, also encompasses herbal medicine. Indeed, the Chinese feel that herbal and food therapy are the primary healing arts, the foundation of all others. The understanding of health and disease and methods of treatment have been developing continuously over about 4,000 years. It rests on the concept of *ch'i*, energy, flowing as yin (the receptive female principle of the universe) and yang (the active male principle of the universe) in currents through the body, and on five elements interacting with each other. Today in China, though Western medical diagnoses and treatments have been adopted, it has not been at the expense of traditional Chinese medicine, which is still highly regarded. Practitioners of each will refer patients to the other. In the West, many herbalists are now specializing in Chinese herbal medicine.

ABOVE HERBS HAVE ALWAYS BEEN IMPORTANT IN CHINESE MEDICINE.

In India, Ayurveda (literally meaning 'the science of life') has similarly survived the onslaught of Western medicine. First written down in Sanskrit some 2,000 years ago, Ayurveda has a distinguished history of healing, including highly advanced surgical techniques, herbal and food therapy, massage, rejuvenation techniques, gemstones and meditation. Diagnoses and treatments are based on principles of *prana* – energy circulating in the body from the subtle regions and manifesting physically as the Five Elements and the Three Humours or Tri Dosha: Vata, Pitta, and Kapha. This tradition is also being successfully brought to the West.

> From Native Americans we learn of another beautiful and profound understanding of natural medicine based on the Great Spirit and the Four Directions: North, South, East and West, each with their particular qualities of energy. These form the Medicine Wheel, within which we are born and journey as we evolve. Here again, herbs play an integral part in the healing process and are valued as guides on this journey.

THE FUTURE

Just as the old knowledge of herbs for healing seemed destined to die out, it has been retrieved and is now growing strongly. Pharmaceutical researchers are investigating the properties of long overlooked herbs and ethno-botanists are consulting aboriginal peoples in Africa and South America about the healing actions of local plants. While much of the research is motivated by the old drive to find and isolate the magical 'active principle', it has at least caused scientists to respect herbal wisdom and to join with environmentalists in calling for the saving of the earth's natural resources.

At the same time, more and more people are using herbs and consulting herbalists. A sea change in the attitude of the medical establishment and governments of western nations means a new openness towards herbal medicine. Herbalists' right to practice is being recognized by governments. Training is independently accredited; standards and ethics established and monitored as with any other health care profession. The public increasingly can reap the benefits of a new model of 'Integrated Medicine' in which both orthodox and complementary practitioners work together in the patient's interest.

RIGHT PHARMACEUTICAL RESEARCHERS NOW APPRECIATE THE HEALING PROPERTIES OF GARLIC.

HOW HERBS HEAL

CHAPTER TWO

Plants are complex living entities. When they are used in healing, they are interacting with another complex living entity, the human body. The body breaks down the plant's identity and assimilates it into its own. This process involves general as well as specific effects, three major areas of bodily function and several different levels of activity.

GENERAL AND SPECIFIC EFFECTS

When using whole herbs, healing is accomplished by a combination of multiple effects. A single herb can interact with several different aspects of the body simultaneously because of its complex energy and variety of biochemical constituents. The body has its own intelligence, or wisdom, and from among the different effects will take what it needs, eliminating the rest safely. Thus, the overall effect of using herbs will be one of regulating bodily activity because they act to support homoeostasis, the body's regulating mechanism. So,

RIGHT HERBS ACT IN CONJUNCTION WITH THE BODY'S INNATE WISDOM, BALANCING AND REGULATING THE FUNCTIONS OF THE BODY.

when used properly, herbal medicine is very unlikely to imbalance the body seriously.

Herbalists consider this a tremendous advantage over drug therapy because while one constituent gives the plant a characteristic action, such as a diuretic one, others are simultaneously affecting other aspects of the body and serve to round out the main action. This multiple effect also means that several herbs may be used successfully for the same ailment, so our range of choice is very wide indeed. The specific therapeutic effects of herbs are described in Chapter Four.

THE TRIAD OF BODILY FUNCTIONS

At any time the body is:

- Breaking down food and air and building new cells and tissues.
- Resting, recuperating and repairing.
- Eliminating waste by-products of metabolism and digestion.

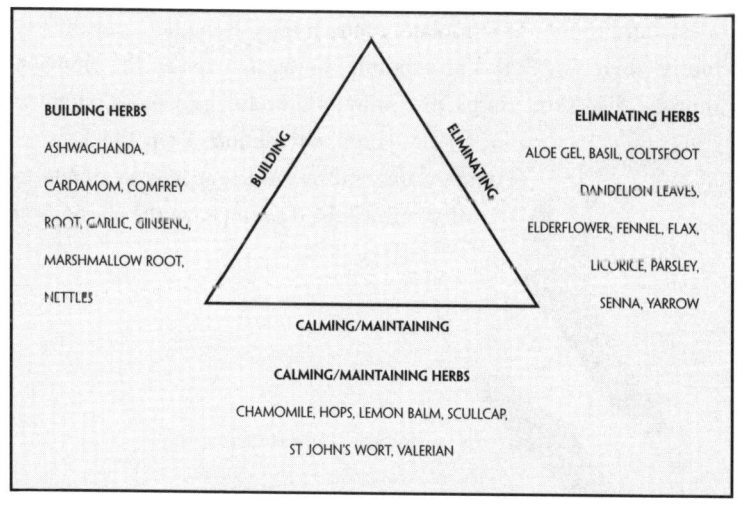

BUILDING HERBS

ASHWAGHANDA, CARDAMOM, COMFREY ROOT, GARLIC, GINSENG, MARSHMALLOW ROOT, NETTLES

ELIMINATING HERBS

ALOE GEL, BASIL, COLTSFOOT, DANDELION LEAVES, ELDERFLOWER, FENNEL, FLAX, LICORICE, PARSLEY, SENNA, YARROW

CALMING/MAINTAINING HERBS

CHAMOMILE, HOPS, LEMON BALM, SCULLCAP, ST JOHN'S WORT, VALERIAN

ABOVE THE TRIAD OF BODILY FUNCTIONS.

LEFT ST JOHN'S WORT IS A CALMING HERB. WHEN USED MEDICINALLY, IT HELPS THE BODY TO RECUPERATE AND RENEW ITS ENERGY.

These three bodily functions form a triad of balanced health, each of which should be roughly equal to the other two. It is an active, dynamic balance adjusting itself constantly in response to the changing inner and outer environment. If the building or the eliminating side becomes either deficient or too dominant, or if there is not adequate rest and repair, then the health of the person suffers. Herbs can be said to nourish, support or activate these three functions and herbalists describe them as building or tonifying, calming and eliminating.

BUILDING

Herbs can improve the body's ability to perform its task of building and strengthening cells and tissues. Certain herbs act on specific organs and tissues to stimulate, nourish and strengthen and thus to 'tonify' their function. For example, herbs that tonify the stomach improve digestion. Herbs that stimulate bodily processes, such as blood and lymph circulation, keep the flow of energy free and ensure that it is available to every cell. Herbs that improve the strength of

LEFT GINSENG IS A RENOWNED ENERGY TONIC. IT IS COMMONLY USED TO TONIFY THE ESSENTIAL ENERGY OF THE BODY.

cells overcome weakness or flaccidity of muscles, nerves and membranes. Some special herbs or herbal combinations have the ability to tonify the essential energy of the body and these are called energy tonics. Ginseng is one such herb.

CALMING

Complete relaxation allows the body to rest and repair, to return to a state of equilibrium, to recover from exertion. This is accomplished primarily through the parasympathetic nervous system (nerves leaving the lower end of the spinal cord connected with those in or near the soft internal organs) in conjunction with the hormones. Over-stimulation or overwork of any organ, tissue or system, will eventually weaken function and undermine health. Even emotional upheavals may lead to stress and tension that can stay locked in the body. Herbs that support the nerves and endocrine glands allow the body to recuperate and renew its energy.

ELIMINATING

Elimination and internal cleansing is as important to health as building. The elimination and cleansing is the responsibility of the kidneys, liver, lungs, skin, lymph and colon. If any one of these systems becomes overburdened by excess and cannot complete its cleansing functions, the body tissues gradually become toxic. Herbs have the ability to enhance the cleansing processes of the body: to break up congestion, neutralize toxins and to promote their elimination. When used in conjunction with good diet, eliminating herbs will keep this important aspect of the health triad fully functioning.

HERBAL ACTIVITY

Herbs affect the body on several different levels simultaneously: the nutritional, biochemical, psycho-emotional and energetic.

THE NUTRITIONAL LEVEL

Many herbs can be used as foods. Others can supply significant quantities of nutrients such as vitamins, minerals and starches. These include lemons, dandelion roots and leaves, burdock roots, nettles and garlic. Herbs can actually be combined to give an excellent mineral and vitamin supplement. Valerian, for example, known for its relaxing effects on the nervous system, contains a high proportion of the mineral calcium needed by the body for healthy nerve function. Consuming herbs regularly in small amounts along with meals helps preserve health and prevent disease.

LEFT A SINGLE LEMON CONTAINS A LARGE AMOUNT OF VITAMINS B AND C.

THE BIOCHEMICAL LEVEL

Plants, whether medicinal herbs or foods, are complex chemical packages. For example, the potato contains over 150 identified substances. The same is true of medicinal herbs. The main active constituents often explain a herb's most characteristic action: tannins, for example, are responsible for astringent, antiseptic and wound-healing actions; some glycosides have sedative, others purgative, effects. But understanding the activity of herbs according to this paradigm is less useful than understanding that a herb is a complex of many different compounds and it is the known therapeutic effects of all these together – the synergistic effect – that is the best guide to its use. (When such active constituents are isolated and given medicinally, as in drug therapy, the strength of their action increases, often dramatically, creating negative side-effects.)

The main medicinally active constituents are the tannins, alkaloids, volatile oils, mucilages, acids, glycosides and bitters. (*See* Further Reading p.122 for additional information on these.)

PSYCHO-EMOTIONAL LEVEL

We have said that herbal medicine aims to treat the whole person, including their mental and emotional aspects. In general, herbs that are cooling and/or heavy are used to ground, calm and sedate. Those that are light and stimulating are used to clear stagnation, uplift and invigorate. For example, when the bloating that can accompany menstruation is reduced, symptoms of irritability and anxiety are relieved. Herbs that are sweet nourish, strengthen and comfort. Aromatic herbs also affect the mental-emotional level and play an important role in the treatment of psycho-emotional problems. Often when congestion and blockages at the physical level are cleared, through the appropriate herbal strategy, mental-emotional clarity and peace are restored.

LEFT LIGHT AND STIMULATING HERBS HAVE A POSITIVE EFFECT ON THE EMOTIONS.

THE ENERGETIC LEVEL

In a sense when we take herbs they are transferring to us the harmonious flow of vital force that they have developed in order to survive, and it is this energy that resolves the disease causing disharmony in ourselves. The recognition of this phenomenon is at the foundation of traditional medicine systems – Tibb (Greek-Islamic), Chinese, Ayurvedic and Native American.

Energetic understanding of herbs is a holistic, comprehensive understanding because it takes into account all dimensions of a plant's nature, not just the biochemical-physical. Understanding the energetics of herbs and how these harmonize the energetic pattern of the particular individual enables us to create the most effective herbal preparations and heal at the deeper levels.

Energy Herbs

The Chinese have a special category of herbs called *ch'i* or energy tonics, which they have found to restore and rebuild the body's life energy. The most famous of these is ginseng. Scientific research on ginseng has provided some clues as to how it works. As Stephen Fulder reports in his book, *About Ginseng*, researchers have found ginseng to have unique and remarkable effects leading them to coin a new term for this class of herbs – 'adaptogens'. Adaptogens increase the body's ability to adapt to stress positively, indeed to survive extremely stressful situations. It is unclear exactly how this occurs, but the plant's action is believed to affect the hormones and nerves, and their response to the environment. In effect, ginseng energizes the whole body.

It is possible that as well as single herbs, certain combinations of herbs may be created whose combined effect also affects energy directly. Several cultures seem to have a famous tonic that is believed to be an elixir of life. One such combination may be Chyavanprash, a highly respected Ayurvedic formula, taken regularly to maintain overall health. As stress is recognized as being an important contributor to many chronic diseases, this new understanding of the abilities of herbs to revitalize is very welcome.

HERBAL ENERGY AND CONSTITUTIONAL TYPES

CHAPTER THREE

The life force expresses itself on the physical level as different qualities or patterns of energy – much as a river has different characteristics and qualities depending on whether it is a rushing mountain stream, a broader lowland river or a wide, silt-laden delta. This expression manifests as the phenomena of Earth, Water, Fire, Air and Ether – substances ranging from the most solid to the most ethereal. These elements are present in differing degrees and combinations in the human body, in plants and throughout nature.

It is significant that each of the major known traditional medical systems of the world developed independent but similar paradigms of energetic understanding to make sense of the natural world, health and disease. These may be described in slightly different terms and configurations of the patterns – perhaps reflecting differences of climate, geographical and cultural experience – but it is sensed that they are descriptions of the same phenomena. In this book, the paradigm of Ayurvedic medicine is chosen as the model. It is very similar to our own European-Greek humoural tradition, includes many herbs in common and has the advantage of still being actively and successfully practised today, after 5,000 years.

THE FIVE ELEMENTS

EARTH

WATER

FIRE

AIR

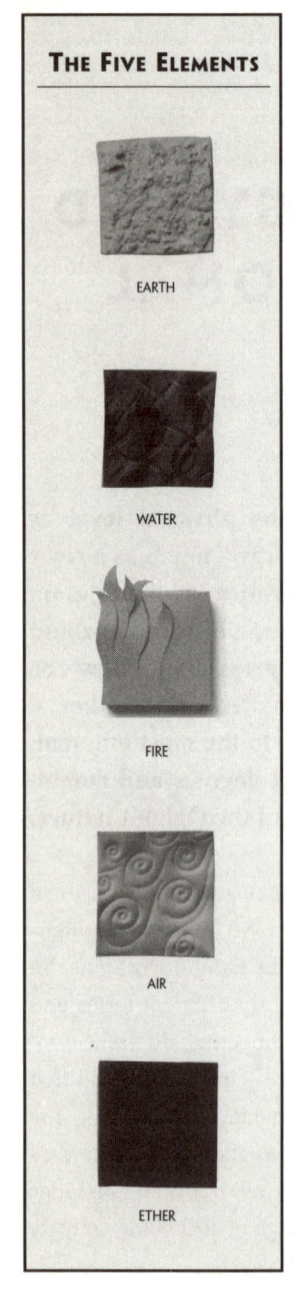

ETHER

THE ELEMENTS

The five elements show different combinations of qualities such as dryness and moisture, heat and cold, lightness and heaviness, mobility and inertia. These are not present in absolute form, but are tendencies within a continuum and are relative to their opposites.

- Earth manifests the qualities of solidity, firmness, heaviness, density and cold.
- Water manifests the qualities of heaviness, fluidity, cold and moisture.
- Fire manifests yet more activity, also heat, light and colour, and less density.
- Air manifests to a greater degree the qualities of mobility, lightness (less weight) and dryness, and also tends to be colder.
- Ether manifests as emptiness, that positive space within which the other elements function, find their expression and communicate or interact with each other. The qualities of ether are clarity and subtlety. At the emotional-mental level, it is the space that allows the free expression of one's true nature. Spiritually, ether is the inner space, emptied of mental activity, wherein the individual consciousness becomes aware of the cosmic spirit. This is the most subtle manifestation of the life force.

Each of these elements is present to greater or lesser extents in all of nature from stones to sub-atomic particles. For example, in humans, Earth would be the most obvious and most characteristic element of bones, teeth and, to a lesser extent, muscles, because these are the most dense and solid tissues in the body. Water is present in great quantities in our bodies but is most obvious in mucous membranes, in the lubricating fluid around joints, in blood and in lymph fluid. Similarly, Fire is manifested in the digestive acids, in that veritable chemical factory, the liver, and in the warmth and redness of blood. Air is represented in the electrical impulses of the nervous system with its qualities of rapid communication and instigation of movement. Even Ether – space – is necessary in the body and is represented in, for example, the thoracic cavities, the colon and the synaptic space through which nerve impulses are transmitted.

In herbs, the elemental energy is expressed in such things as the earthiness of bark and roots; the fluidity of sap; the fire of colour in flowers and the chemical process of photosynthesis; the breathing of air by leaves; and the space within which the seed forms.

Herbs and their Energetic Qualities

Four main qualities characterize herbs: warmth, coolness, dryness and moistness. These describe the energy effect herbs have in the body as cooling, warming, drying or moistening, some herbs being more cooling or warming than others.

Warming herbs stimulate metabolism, adding heat, and stimulate the body's energy. But a very heating herb will also have a drying effect if used for long enough, and eventually a depleting effect if the body is over-stimulated, so it is recommended more for short-term use in those with dry symptoms, Air imbalance or weakness.

Cooling herbs counteract excess heat in the body – fevers or inflammations. They help the elimination or clearing of heat through the sweat glands, kidneys, liver or colon.

Moistening herbs, often barks or roots with a starchy, fibrous or soft texture, impart a demulcent, softening, soothing effect to dry, inflamed or irritated tissues and strengthen the basic fluid essence of the body, the Water humour.

Drying herbs are either astringent in effect – drying excess water in tissues by a tightening, binding action – or stimulating to the urinary and circulatory systems, which increases the elimination of water via skin or the kidneys. They are good for excess damp conditions such as swellings and catarrh. Herbs can exhibit two qualities at the same time, though one may tend to be its primary effect.

THE THREE HUMOURS AND THE CONSTITUTIONAL TYPES

In the body the elements of Earth, Water, Fire, Air and Ether mingle to create three distinct patterns of energy, or 'humours' as they are called in Ayurvedic and Greek-Tibb medicine. (These three humours correspond roughly to the concepts of Yin, Yang and Wind in Chinese medicine.) As all the five elements are present in each of us, so are each of the three humours, but in varying degrees. The predominant ones indicate our predispositions, our constitutional type or our temperament.

THE THREE HUMOURS

Earth and Water together constitute the Water humour (*kapha*). Fire combines with some degree of Water's fluidity to constitute the Fire humour (*pitta*). Air and Ether taken together constitute the Air humour (*vata*). Like the elements, the humours are expressed in the body's anatomy and physiology; for example, digestion and circulation relate primarily to the Fire humour, mucous and urine to the Water humour and nerves and movement to the Air humour. The humours also find expression at the more subtle level of emotional and mental make-up.

CONSTITUTIONAL TYPES

Some of us are born with a tendency to be strong in one humour, others perhaps in two and some may have a more even distribution of humours. We may be a Water-predominant type, a Fire type or an Air type; or perhaps a Water-Fire, Earth-Air or Fire-Air type. The characteristic temperament at birth may become modified, imbalanced or even obscured by life's experiences and activities such as emotional traumas, diet, exercise or lifestyle. Our particular mix of humours can also predispose us to certain types of illness when we become unbalanced. This is because the predominant humour will also be the one to most easily tip into excess and cause imbalance, though any of the humours can become imbalanced given a particular set of negative circumstances in our lives.

Each humour can act as either a positive or negative factor in our lives depending on whether or not it is in balance with the other two and with our current environment – just as we need a certain amount of physical fire in our bodies for warmth but not so much as to dry out our tissues. Similarly, there may be times when we need to become a little fiery in order to defend ourselves, both physiologically – the immune response of the body is a function of the fire energy – and emotionally. At other times, we need to express love or find new ways of thinking and responding in order to change and develop – aspects of the Water and Air humours. The positive quality of each humour indicates the one to activate and support with herbs and food when restoring harmony.

We all have each of the humours within us and each will manifest more strongly at different stages of life or given enough imbalance. For simplicity's sake those constitutional types described here are of only one main humour dominance. Childhood and winter are typically the time of the Water humour; youth and adulthood, spring and summer are the time of the Fire humour; older age and autumn the time of the Air humour. Although Water types are more inclined to experience phlegm and mucous excess, over-exposure to cold and damp can imbalance the Water humour in other types too.

Water Type

A Water-type person tends to be strong, steady and calm, compassionate and placid. He may need financial security, and seems to attract it, and may be quite attached to loved ones. On the physical level, this type will be of heavier build and prone to overweight, water retention or respiratory congestion. Over-concern, stagnation, introversion, depression or rigidity of attitude are the negative aspects of the Water humour.

Herbs for Water types include warming, metabolic stimulants such as cayenne, black pepper, thyme, rosemary, garlic, sage and eucalyptus; draining herbs such as juniper, chickweed, cleavers and dandelion; and dispersing herbs such as basil and yarrow. Water types should avoid sweet and rich or processed foods, as well as salt.

Fire Type

A Fire-type person tends to be perceptive, goal-oriented, efficient and practical. She knows her own mind. On the physical level, she will have good digestive fire, warm circulation and a medium body-build. Of the three constitutions, the Fire type is the most prone to digestive problems such as acidity or heartburn, heavy menstrual periods or skin complaints, as it is easiest for this type to become imbalanced by additional heat – whether mental, emotional or physical. The Fire type is also most easily irritable, angry and will tend to overwork.

Herbs for Fire types or imbalanced Fire include cooling herbs or neutral herbs such as coriander, cumin, turmeric, borage, burdock, red clover, licorice, asparagus. Avoid too much heating, spicy herbs such as chillies, and sour, fried and salty foods.

Air Type

The Air-type person tends to be flexible in mind and body, especially sensitive to surroundings and change and quick to react to new things. The

RIGHT DANDELION IS A DIURETIC AND CAN BE USEFUL FOR IMBALANCED WATER.

keynote for her is variation and irregularity. The Air type tends to a lighter frame, less substance and to feel cold, preferring warmth and light. She can be excited and intensely active, then tire and need rest. When imbalanced, physical symptoms may be those of stiffness, nervousness or hyperactivity, dryness or lack of energy and endurance. On the mental-emotional level, imbalance shows as indecisiveness, feelings of anxiety, insecurity or lack of confidence.

Herbs for Air types or imbalanced Air include grounding, relaxing or warming herbs such as valerian, chamomile, catnip and ginger; and tonic or moistening herbs such as comfrey, dong quai, licorice, slippery elm, kelp, honey, fenugreek, oats and oatstraw.

Constitutional Type Assessment

Awareness of one's constitutional make-up leads to a greater understanding and acceptance of oneself and of others. We realize why a particular food – or even a person – upsets us: it is probably because it aggravates a particular humour or tendency in us. We can discern the best food, herb or activity that will restore harmony. The awareness gives positive guidance in how to minimize our limitations and make the most of our strengths by seeing them in the context of the overall dynamic flow of energy in us.

For this purpose, use the Humour Assessment table on pp.34–35. It will enable you to know yourself, your strengths and weaknesses and your tendencies when imbalance occurs. Herbs may then be chosen more accurately to restore or maintain your balance. Tick the column that best describes your overall tendency in each category throughout your life in general, not just most recently. You will find different aspects of yourself fall under each humour, which is normal. Add up the number of ticks in each column; the results will give you a good idea of the strength of each humour in yourself. Repeat the assessment at intervals.

Table 1 Humour Assessment

	WATER (EARTH AND WATER)	FIRE (WATER AND FIRE)	AIR (AIR AND ETHER)
STRUCTURE (PHYSIQUE)	STURDY. LARGE BONES, CHEST. TENDS TO OVERWEIGHT.	MEDIUM BUILD AND WEIGHT.	SLENDER. SMALL CHEST. LIGHT OR UNDERWEIGHT.
HAIR	THICK, ABUNDANT, OFTEN WAVY. MORE BODY HAIR.	OILY, STRAIGHT, BLONDE, RED. TENDS TO BALDNESS.	FINE, DARK. CAN BE KINKY (IRREGULAR).
SKIN	MOIST, SOFT, FAIR TO PALE, THICK, COOL.	MOIST, OILY. TENDS TO MOLES, FRECKLES, BIRTH MARKS, ACNE.	PATCHY DRY OR ROUGH, THIN, DARK, COLD. VEINS PROMINENT.
APPETITE	MODERATE, STEADY. PREFERS SWEET TASTING FOODS.	STRONG. NEEDS FOOD TO BE CONTENT AND TO WORK.	VARIABLE, BUT FEELS 'SPACEY' WITHOUT FOOD.
DIGESTION	SLUGGISH. FOOD 'SITS' IN STOMACH.	EFFICIENT, FAST. TENDS TO ACIDITY.	IRREGULAR, WORSE WITH CHANGE OR TRAVEL.
EXERCISE AND MOVEMENT	MOVES SLOWLY OR WITH RELUCTANCE, SEDENTARY. PREFERS SLOWNESS, CONSERVES ENERGY.	ACTIVE, PREFERS COMPETITIVE SPORTS.	ACTIVE BUT TENDS TO RESTLESSNESS OR TOSSING, NERVOUS MOVEMENT.
STAMINA AND ENERGY	STRONG. SLOWER TO START BUT STEADY. GOOD ENDURANCE.	MODERATE. FOCUSES ENERGY. TENDS TO OVERWORK.	LOW OR FLUCTUATING. QUICK TO START AND TO STOP. INTENSE ENERGY, THEN FATIGUE.
STOOLS	MODERATELY FREQUENT, HEAVY WITH MUCUS. TENDS TO SLUGGISHNESS.	REGULAR (ONE OR MORE A DAY), LARGE, SOFT, YELLOW-TINGED.	VARIABLE, AFFECTED BY SLIGHT CHANGE (E.G. TRAVEL). TENDS TO DRYNESS, HARDNESS OR CONSTIPATION.
SWEAT	MODERATE.	EASILY PRODUCED, PROFUSE. SENSITIVE TO HEAT.	LITTLE, NOT EASILY PROVOKED.

	WATER (EARTH AND WATER)	**FIRE** (WATER AND FIRE)	**AIR** (AIR AND ETHER)
URINE	MODERATE. TENDS TO MILKY COLOUR.	PROFUSE. CAN BE RED OR BURNING WHEN IMBALANCED.	SCANTY, LESS COLOUR.
CIRCULATION AND BODY TEMPERATURE	MODERATE TO COOL. LEAST SENSITIVE TO CHANGES. COPES WELL WITH EXTREMES (E.G. OF HEAT AND COLD).	STRONG, FEELS WARM. SENSITIVE TO HEAT.	FEELS COLD, AND FEELS 'THE COLD'. DISTURBED BY UNEVEN TEMPERATURES, CHANGES, WIND.
SLEEP	SOUND. ENJOYS LONG SLEEP. SLOW TO WAKEN. TENDS TO EXCESS.	MODERATE, UNINTERRUPTED. MIND CONTROLS SLEEP, 'NIGHT OWL'.	LIGHT. EASILY DISTURBED, WAKES EARLY. MORNING IS BEST TIME.
DREAMS	ROMANTIC, EMOTIONAL.	COLOURFUL, INVOLVE CONFLICT, PASSION.	ACTIVE. INVOLVE MOVEMENT E.G. FLIGHT, FALLING.
MENTAL, EMOTIONAL AND LIFESTYLE	THINKS SLOWLY, CAREFULLY. RETAINS WELL. GOOD ADMINISTRATOR. COMPASSIONATE, DEVOTED, PATIENT, CALM, OVERLY PRUDENT, SENTIMENTAL. DESIRES SECURITY (E.G. FINANCIAL, LOVE).	SHARP, PENETRATING, PRACTICAL, ARTICULATE, KNOWS OWN MIND. CLARITY OF THOUGHT. AVID READER, LIKES TO BE BUSY, COMPETITIVE, AMBITIOUS, JUDGEMENTAL. TEACHER, LEADER.	OPEN MIND. ALERT, QUICK TO LEARN AND TO FORGET; TO GRASP AND TO REJECT. TALKATIVE, ACTIVE, TENDS TO BE RESTLESS AND SENSITIVE, ENJOYS TRAVEL AND CHANGE. FLEXIBLE. COMMUNICATOR.
MOST LIKELY NEGATIVE EMOTION	GRIEF	ANGER	ANXIETY AND FEAR.
AREAS OF FOCUS OF IMBALANCES	RESPIRATORY, MUCOUS CONGESTION, INERTIA, WATER RETENTION, WEIGHT GAIN.	DIGESTIVE, LIVER, SKIN. FEVERS, INFLAMMATIONS. IRRITABILITY.	INSOMNIA, STIFFNESS, NERVOUS OR MENTAL DISTRESS.
TOTALS			

THE THERAPEUTIC ACTIONS OF HERBS

CHAPTER FOUR

Any herb produces several of the therapeutic actions that may simultaneously affect the body and that are moderated by that body's energetic pattern. A knowledge of the main actions described here, combined with a knowledge of humoural constitution, or temperament, will allow you to form a successful herbal strategy.

DIGESTIVE ACTION

This action affects the digestion and assimilation of foods and the elimination of digestive residues such as gas. Carminatives are usually flavourful and include many of our common spices and seasonings. They are also effective medicines for digestive and intestinal symptoms.

In Water temperaments, their digestive fire is liable to be low or sluggish and they benefit from the most warming carminatives such as ginger, pepper and garlic. In Fire types, the tendency is for the

LEFT CLOVES ARE WARMING AND SWEET AND WILL BENEFIT AIR TYPES, WHO TEND TO HAVE VARIABLE DIGESTION AND EATING HABITS.

digestive fire to be a little too high, so the mild carminatives, such as cumin and fennel, are helpful. In Air types, digestion and eating habits tend to be variable; they benefit most from warming and sweet carminatives such as ginger, cinnamon and cloves. Digestive bitters, such as yellow gentian root, while not pleasantly flavourful like carminatives, stimulate the digestive enzymes, tonify the stomach, and therefore improve overall health, especially in cases of ulcers, weakness or debility.

LAXATIVE ACTION

This action regulates and balances good bowel elimination. Some of these herbs stimulate metabolism, some moisten and soften the contents, adding bulk, some tone the smooth muscles or stimulate the gall bladder to release bile, the body's natural laxative.

Ginger or cayenne would most benefit Water types: rosemary combined with slippery elm in milk would help Fire types; ginger with psyllium seed, flax seed or aloe vera would work well for Air types. Raspberry and rosemary tonify the peristaltic muscles. If any cramping or griping effect is experienced when taking laxative herbs, combine them with warming antispasmodic herbs (*see* Nervine Action, p.41).

BLOOD-PURIFYING ACTION

This action – also called alterative, heat clearing and Fire reducing – clears excess heat in the blood and body. Excess heat may be caused by pathogens such as bacteria, viruses, accumulated food, chemical poisons or poisonous bites or stings. If not neutralized in the liver, such toxicity can accumulate and eventually pass to organs and tissues to produce symptoms such as fever, inflammation, infection, skin problems and sepsis. It can play a part in arthritis and is a factor in cancer and AIDS. The alterative action cools the blood either directly by killing the pathogens or indirectly by purifying and strengthening the liver and lymphatic system and by increasing the number and activity of the body's own immune cells. Demulcent alternatives such as marshmallow root soothe irritations and counteract inflammations.

DIAPHORETIC ACTION

This action is also known as sudorific and these herbs promote sweating and the expulsion of toxicity through the skin. Diaphoretic herbs relieve fevers associated with colds and flu, as well as coughs and mild asthma, skin eruptions, superficial oedema, body aches and stiffness, especially upper parts, arthritis, excess weight, swellings and fluid retention. The herbs conduct the circulation of energy from the centre to the surface, and disperse stagnation. Their use is indicated for chills, colds and excess water, but the cooling ones are contraindicated for excess Air imbalances where the individual, no matter what constitutional type, is weak and emaciated (dry and cold). The warming diaphoretic herbs are best avoided with very excessive heat or inflammatory conditions.

EXPECTORANT ACTION

This action assists the body to remove excess phlegm, mucous or catarrh congesting the lungs, sinuses and nasal passages and ears. Some expectorants help liquify and soften the phlegm and provide lubrication so that it is more easily expelled. Some provide warmth to help dry and eliminate it, and some stimulate elimination and disperse congestion.

Although manifesting in the lungs, a fundamental cause of acute excess mucous is most likely to lie in the stomach with poor digestion. To resolve the situation fully, herbal remedies would also include carminatives and circulatory stimulants. Avoiding mucous-forming foods such as dairy products, eggs, meat and refined flour products also helps.

Fire types or excess heat show signs such as inflammation with cloudy, yellow, fairly loose catarrh. Use cooling herbs such as comfrey, coltsfoot, pleurisy root, nettles and violet leaves. Water types or excess Water show signs of sinus congestion, leading to

LEFT ECHINACEA CAN BE USED IN CONDITIONS WHERE THERE IS INFLAMMATION.

headaches with clear, congesting phlegm. Use warming and/or drying herbs such as ginger, pepper or garlic combined with a carminative and a diuretic herb, to promote the elimination of excess damp. Air types or excess Air show a dry, or unproductive cough with fatigue, perhaps brought on by chill, stress or anxiety or fatigue. Use warming herbs combined with demulcent herbs to soften mucous and lubricate membranes and herbs to relax and nourish the nervous system (*see* Nervine Action, p.41). In mixed types, choose herbs according to both symptoms and constitutional type.

If there is inflammation, add anti-inflammatory and soothing herbs such as echinacea, slippery elm or marshmallow root.

Whenever there are symptoms of blood in the sputum, extreme dryness in nose and throat, continued or repeated fever or inflammation, or weakness, fatigue and a thin watery mucous discharge, these indicate a more complex and deeper problem and professional advice should be sought.

DIURETIC ACTION

This action benefits the urinary system, improving the excretion of urine while at the same time nourishing the urinary organs and promoting balanced water and mineral metabolism at the cellular level. Common ailments of the urinary system include kidney stones, cystitis, urinary tract infections, painful burning sensations, swelling of the prostate, excess uric acid, incontinence and retention of urine. Even lower backache may be related to poor kidney function.

BLOOD-REGULATING AND EMMENAGOGUE ACTION

This action affects the circulation and movement of blood, the liquid tissue of the body, promoting its efficient, smooth and correctly channelled flow. When there is either congestion or injury to the body, this will in some way affect the blood flow, causing either stagnation or haemorrhaging. Therapeutic blood regulating action helps with blood or circulation problems – such as menstrual irregularity or discomfort, anaemia, weakness, cold, stroke or hypertension – as well as trauma to tissues from wounds, sprains or operations. It promotes healing, prevents sepsis and clears the bruising.

Warming blood regulators include thyme, angelica, garlic, turmeric, myrrh and dong quai; cooling ones include comfrey, motherwort, yarrow, shepherd's purse and raspberry. Tonifying blood regulators include nettles, dong quai, yarrow and myrrh; raspberry is particularly tonifying to the uterus. Relaxing ones include dong quai, angelica, thyme, marjoram and shepherd's purse. Herbs to arrest bleeding include cayenne, comfrey, shepherd's purse and turmeric.

LEFT THE CIRCULATORY SYSTEM MAY BE REGULATED AND STIMULATED BY HERBS SUCH AS ANGELICA AND DONG QUAI.

DEMULCENT ACTION

This action has a very special quality to it: as these herbs combine with water, they become moist, soft and dense. When they meet body tissue they impart these qualities to it and soothe irritated, inflamed, swollen, 'angry' tissue – whether externally as a skin problem, or internally as perhaps an irritable bowel. Demulcent herbs calm inordinate heat of urinary infections, burns or sore throats, and sweet, moistening herbs such as licorice and red clover will nourish the Water essence needed in cases of extreme dryness, wasting, emaciation, weakness or fatigue.

RIGHT TURMERIC CAN REGULATE THE BLOOD AND ALSO HELP TO STOP BLEEDING.

ASTRINGENT ACTION

This action has a condensing, tightening and drying effect on tissues, and is commonly used to treat symptoms of acute fluid elimination such as runny or bleeding noses, diarrhoea, internal and external bleeding, discharge of pus and vaginal discharge. It is also used to tone flaccid muscles, mucous membranes or cell walls. It is important that symptomatic treatment should always be combined with herbs to redress the underlying causes of the condition.

NERVINE ACTION

Nervine action affects the nervous system and through it the entire body. Nervine herbs are antispasmodic and will release muscular tension, both conscious and unconscious, reduce and relieve pain by their analgesic and sedative action, and calm nerves and induce relaxation and sleep. Some nervine herbs can nourish nerve tissues, strengthening the system generally and counteracting stress. Some have a lightening quality that lifts lowered spirits while calming anxiety, and some an earthy quality that grounds nervous excitability and spaciness.

LEFT COMFREY HAS ASTRINGENT PROPERTIES.

TONIFYING ACTION

This action includes more than may at first be apparent. In addition to strengthening individual organs and tissues, tonifying restores the body generally to strength and vitality and, used regularly, maintains a vibrant level. By nourishing tissues and energy, it helps combat disease, increases immunity and enhances the quality of life.

Tonifying herbs are especially indicated where there is emaciation, debility or weakness. However, the more assertive ones such as ginseng or juniper should be avoided during an acute crisis such as a fever, infection, inflammation, cold or flu because the strength of the herb will tend to add strength to the illness.

WOUND-HEALING ACTION

This action promotes the regrowth of new cells and healing of traumatized tissue. The herbs have soothing, antiseptic, astringent and blood regulating properties – bringing blood to the site when needed but also preventing haemorrhaging and blood stasis. Used internally as well as externally, they heal bruises and abrasions and deeper traumatized tissues such as sprains, torn ligaments, dry or emaciated tissue, weakened vertebrae and broken bones.

LEFT NERVINE HERBS WORK ON THE NERVOUS SYSTEM, REDUCING PAIN AND INDUCING RELAXATION.

THE THERAPEUTIC ACTIONS OF HERBS

HERBAL ENERGETICS AND THERAPEUTIC ACTIONS

HERBS/FOOD	ENERGY: NEUTRAL / WARMING / COOLING / DRYING / MOISTENING		CARMINATIVE	LAXATIVE	DIAPHORETIC	DIURETIC	EXPECTORANT	DEMULCENT	ASTRINGENT	BLOOD PURIFYING	NERVINE	BLOOD REGULATING	TONIFYING	VULNERARY	HUMOUR: INCREASES ↑ / DECREASES ↓ / MIXED OR NEUTRAL ⇔ / AIR, FIRE, WATER
Kitchen Herbs															
ALLSPICE	W	D	●		●					●	●		●		F↑ W↓ A↓
ANISE	W	D	●		●		●			●	●				F↑ W↓ A↓
BASIL	W	D	●		●		●					●	●		F↑ W↓ A↓
BAY	W	D	●		●							●			F↑ W↓ A↓
BLACK PEPPER	W	D	●				●								F↑ W↓ A↓
CARAWAY	W		●												F↑ W↓ A↓
CARDAMOM	W		●				●						●		F↑ W↓ A↓
CAYENNE	W	D	●		●					●	●		●		F↑ W↓ A↑
CINNAMON	W	D	●		●					●	●				F↑ W↓ A↓
CLOVES	W	D	●				●				●				F↑ W↓ A⇔
CORIANDER	C-N		●			●									F, W, A⇔
CUMIN	C		●			●									F, W, A⇔
FENNEL	C	M	●	●		●	●	●					●		F, W, A⇔
FENUGREEK	W	M	●		●		●	●		●			●		F↑ W↓ A↓
GARLIC	W	D	●		●		●			●		●	●	●	F↑ W↓ A↓
GINGER	W	D	●		●						●	●			F↑ W↓ A⇔
HONEY	W	D					●	●				●	●	●	F↑ W↓ A↓
HORSERADISH	W		●		●		●			●					F↑ W↓ A↓
LEMON JUICE	C		●				●		●	●	●		●		F↓ W⇔ A↓
MARJORAM (OREGANO)	W		●		●							●			F↑ W↓ A↓
MUNG BEANS	N	M				●				●			●		F⇔ W↓ A↓
MUSTARD	W	D	●		●		●			●					F↑ W↓ A↓
NUTMEG	W	D	●						●		●				F↑ W↓ A↓
OATS/OATSTRAW	N			●				●			●		●		F↓ W↑ A↓
OIL (OLIVE, SESAME)	N	M		●				●					●		F⇔ W↑ A⇔
ONION	W					●				●					F↑ W↓ A↓
PARSLEY	W		●			●				●					F↑ W↓ A↓
ROSEMARY	W		●		●		●		●	●	●	●	●		F↑ W↓ A↓
SAGE	W	D			●		●		●	●		●	●		F↑ W↓ A↓
THYME	W		●		●		●			●	●	●	●		F↑ W↓ A↓

HERBAL REMEDIES

HERBS/FOOD	ENERGY NEUTRAL WARMING COOLING DRYING MOISTENING		CARMINATIVE	LAXATIVE	DIAPHORETIC	DIURETIC	EXPECTORANT	DEMULCENT	ASTRINGENT	BLOOD PURIFYING	NERVINE	BLOOD REGULATING	TONIFYING	VULNERARY	HUMOUR INCREASES ↑ DECREASES ↓ MIXED OR NEUTRAL ⇔ AIR, FIRE, WATER
Kitchen Herbs cont.															
TURMERIC	W		●							●	●		●	●	F⇔ W↓ A↓
VINEGAR, APPLE CIDER	C	D	●							●	●				F↑ W↓ A⇔
Garden Herbs															
ALOE	C	M		●				●	●	●				●	REGULATES ALL
BORAGE	C		●		●		●	●			●	●			F↑ W↓ A⇔
CATNIP	C		●		●						●	●			F↓ W↓ A⇔
CHAMOMILE	C-N		●		●						●	●			F↓ W↓ A⇔
CORNSILK	C					●		●							F↓ W↓ A⇔
DONG QUAI	W				●					●	●	●	●		REGULATES ALL
ELDERFLOWER	C				●	●	●				●				F↓ W↓ A⇔
ELECAMPANE	W		●			●	●		●				●		F↑ W↓ A↓
FEVERFEW	C		●							●					F↓ W↓ A⇔
GINSENG	W										●	●	●	●	TONES WFA
HEARTSEASE (PANSY)	C				●	●	●			●	●	●		●	F↓ W↓ A⇔
HIBISCUS	C					●			●			●			F↓ W↓ A↑
HOLLYHOCK	C	M					●	●		●			●		F↓ W↑ A↓
HONEYSUCKLE	C				●	●				●	●				F↓ W↓ A↑
HYSSOP	W	D			●		●			●			●		F↑ W↓ A↓
JUNIPER	W	D	●			●				●			●		F↑ W↓ A↓
LADY'S MANTLE	N									●		●			F↓ W↓ A⇔
LAVENDER	W					●				●	●	●			F↓ W↓ A⇔
LEMON BALM	C		●		●						●	●			F↓ W↓ A⇔
MARIGOLD	C				●			●		●		●		●	F↓ W↓ A↑
NASTURTIUM	W		●							●					F↑ W↓ A↓
PEONY	C									●	●	●	●	●	F↑ W↓ A⇔
PEPPERMINT	C-W		●		●					●					F↓ W↓ A⇔
PERIWINKLE	N								●		●	●			F↓ W↓ A⇔
SKULLCAP	C									●	●				F↓ W↓ A⇔
ST JOHN'S WORT	C							●	●	●	●		●	●	F↓ W↓ A⇔
VERVAIN	C				●	●				●	●	●	●	●	F↓ W↓ A⇔
VIOLET	C						●	●			●	●			F↓ W↓ A⇔
WALNUT LEAF	C								●	●				●	F↑ W↓ A↓

THE THERAPEUTIC ACTIONS OF HERBS

HERBS/FOOD	ENERGY (NEUTRAL, WARMING, COOLING, DRYING, MOISTENING)		CARMINATIVE	LAXATIVE	DIAPHORETIC	DIURETIC	EXPECTORANT	DEMULCENT	ASTRINGENT	BLOOD PURIFYING	NERVINE	BLOOD REGULATING	TONIFYING	VULNERARY	HUMOUR (INCREASES ↑ DECREASES ↓ MIXED OR NEUTRAL ⇔ AIR, FIRE, WATER)
Garden Herbs cont.															
WOOD BETONY	C									●	●		●	●	F↓ W↓ A⇔
Wild Herbs															
AGRIMONY	W					●				●	●	●		●	F↓ W↓ A⇔
BARBERRY	C			●						●			●		F↓ W↓ A⇔
BIRCH TWIGS	W				●	●			●	●	●				F↓ W↓ A⇔
BISTORT	C				●				●	●		●			F↓ W↓ A↑
BLUE FLAG IRIS	C			●		●				●			●		F↓ W↓ A↑
BURDOCK	C				●	●			●	●			●		F↓ W↓ A↑
CALAMUS, SWEET	W		●								●		●		F↑ W↓ A↓
CHICKWEED	C					●	●		●	●				●	F↓ W↓ A⇔
CLEAVERS	C	D				●		●			●				F↓ W↓ A↑
COLTSFOOT	C-N						●	●	●						F↓ W↓ A⇔
COMFREY	C					●	●	●	●	●		●	●	●	F↓ W↑ A↓
COUCH GRASS	C					●		●							F↓ W↓ A⇔
DANDELION	C		●			●				●			●		F↓ W↓ A↑
ECHINACEA	C									●			●		F↓ W↓ A↑
EPHEDRA	W				●		●			●	●				F↑ W↓ A↑
EYEBRIGHT	C							●	●	●					F↓ W↓ A↑
FLAX SEED	N	M		●			●	●		●	●				BALANCES ALL
GENTIAN, YELLOW	C		●										●		F↓ W↓ A↑
GOLDEN SEAL	C			●		●			●	●			●	●	F↓ W↓ A↑
GROUND IVY	W		●		●			●	●					●	F↑ W↓ A↓
HAWTHORN	W		●								●	●	●		F↑ W⇔ A↓
HEATHER	N						●				●		●		F, W, A⇔
HOPS	C		●								●		●		F↓ W↑ A↑
HORSETAIL	C	D				●			●					●	F↓ W↓ A↑
IRISH MOSS	W	M		●			●	●		●			●		F↑ W↑ A↓
KELP	C	M				●	●	●		●			●		F↑ W↑ A↓
KUDZU	C	M	●		●			●					●		F↓ W↑ A↓
LICORICE	N	M	●	●			●	●			●		●		F↓ W↑ A↓
MARSHMALLOW	C	M			●		●	●	●				●	●	F↓ W↑ A↓
MEADOWSWEET	C	D		●	●		●	●		●					F↓ W↓ A⇔

HERBAL REMEDIES

HERBS/FOOD	ENERGY		THERAPEUTIC ACTION												HUMOUR
	NEUTRAL WARMING COOLING DRYING MOISTENING		CARMINATIVE	LAXATIVE	DIAPHORETIC	DIURETIC	EXPECTORANT	DEMULCENT	ASTRINGENT	BLOOD PURIFYING	NERVINE	BLOOD REGULATING	TONIFYING	VULNERARY	INCREASES ↑ DECREASES ↓ MIXED OR NEUTRAL ↔ AIR, FIRE, WATER
Wild Herbs cont.															
MISTLETOE LEAF	W										●	●			F↑ W↓ A↓
MOTHERWORT	W		●			●			●		●		●		F↔ W↓ A↑
MULLEIN	C						●	●			●			●	F↓ W↓ A↑
NETTLE	C					●	●		●	●		●	●		F↓ W↓ A↑
PASSIONFLOWER	C										●				F↓ W↓ A↔
PLANTAIN	C					●			●	●				●	F↓ W↓ A↑
RASPBERRY/STRAWBERRY	C								●	●			●		F↓ W↓ A↑
RED CLOVER	C							●		●	●		●		F↓ W↓ A↑
ROSEHIP	N–W		●						●				●		F↑ W↑ A↓
SELF-HEAL	N–C				●				●	●		●		●	F↓ W↓ A↑
SHEPHERD'S PURSE	C				●				●	●		●		●	F↓ W↓ A↑
SKULLCAP	C										●		●		F↓ W↓ A↔
SLIPPERY ELM	N	M					●	●	●				●	●	F↓ W↑ A↓
SQUAW VINE	C				●				●			●			F↓ W↓ A↑
UVA-URSI (BEARBERRY)	C				●				●						F↓ W↓ A↑
VALERIAN	W		●			●					●		●		F↑ W↓ A↓
WHITE PINE	W	D			●		●								F↑ W↑ A↓
WHITE WILLOW	C								●	●	●				F↓ W↓ A↑
YARROW	C		●		●	●	●		●		●	●	●	●	F↓ W↓ A↑
YELLOW DOCK	C				●				●	●			●		F↓ W↓ A↑

HANDS-ON HERBS

CHAPTER FIVE

Gathering Your Herbs

Wandering the country lanes or forests, or walking through a garden gathering herbs, is a delight and adventure as well as a restoring of the soul – a therapy in itself. Try to gather from a site at least 100 yards from the nearest main road or field, and several miles from an industrial site to avoid plants that have become contaminated with chemical pollutants.

Guidelines for Gathering Plants

Wear protective clothing and, if necessary, gloves; carry a large bag and some secateurs. Take a strong root stick or garden fork for digging roots and a small axe if cutting bark.

RIGHT YOU WILL NEED SOME BASIC EQUIPMENT FOR GATHERING HERBS.

MINDFULNESS

The best way to gather your herbs is to adopt the practice of the Native Americans. When gathering, they take only from a place where the plant is growing in profusion and, before cutting, they offer words of appreciation and thanks to the plant and to the spirit for the healing gift within it. They never take more than one third of the plants within a group, nor more than one third of each particular plant, unless, of course, it is a single rooted plant such as the dandelion.

IDENTIFICATION

Whether in the wild or the garden, be sure that you can accurately identify the exact species of the plants you want. Take a good identification guide along, and if there is any doubt, do not gather.

TIMING

Gather your herbs when the life energy of the plant is at its most expressive or developed and the therapeutic properties most concentrated. Be guided by these general principles:

- Gather your herbs when the plants are dry – that is, not after a rain or in heavy dew.

- Gather plant parts before the sun is at its height, especially when gathering aromatic parts, as the sun's warmth will at first draw out but later reduce the aromatic molecules as it gets hotter.

- Gather the desired plant part in which the medicinal properties are most concentrated (indicated in the Materia Medica) at the season when it is at its peak. For example, early spring is the best time to collect the medicinal roots or rhizomes, such as dandelion, burdock, elecampane, yellow dock and angelica.

- If gathering the leaves and flowering stem, or the flower itself, collect them when they are fresh. The leaves of some plants, such as lavender, lemon balm, hyssop, rosemary and sage, are collected just before the plant flowers. Sometimes only the flowering heads are wanted and as these continue to flower they can be gathered periodically. Such herbs include marigold, rose and borage. Pick the flowers just as they are opening fully.

- If the properties you require are concentrated in the seeds or fruit, collect in late summer or autumn when they are ripe; for example, fennel seeds, hawthorn berries and rosehips.

- Collecting medicinal barks from shrubs and trees such as peach, slippery elm and cramp bark is best when the sap has just come into that part, either in spring when it is rising or in autumn when it is flowing back towards the root.

HARVESTING

Having chosen the specimen, and the time and place for collecting, use the following guidelines for harvesting.

- Only gather from places where there is an abundance of the plant. Do not take more than you need and never more than one small amount of the population. Never gather from a plant that is a threatened or protected species.

- When gathering the aerial parts, only cut them from the top one-third of the stem and never take more than one-third of the stems or flowers. For roots, it is of course necessary to dig the whole root. For seeds, it is best to cut the stem just below the seed head and take it home intact. Cut flowering heads just beneath the florets.

- Always collect bark from a branch, not the main trunk, and never remove the bark in a full circle around it. Instead, cut a rectangular area of the outer bark, about one-third of the way around, and remove this. Alternatively, cut a branch that needs pruning, then scrape off or cut away just the inner, living cambium layer; do not go deeply into the tree. Or, collect the twigs and small branches of the tree in spring when the sap has risen, as if pruning the tree. Take the inner bark and cut it up before drying.

- When taking the inner bark of roots, having gathered them whole, scrape away the thin outer layer and collect the inner bark.

RESPONSIBLE GATHERING

The demand for herbs is growing with the popularity of herbal medicine, and all herbs should be gathered wild from uncontaminated sites. However, this can threaten the very existence of some species. In North America, the gathering of ginseng, golden seal, and trillium since the 18th and 19th centuries and now echinacea in the 20th has greatly reduced the range of these herbs. Similar situations already exist, or soon will, in other countries. When buying products, enquire how the raw materials are obtained. For personal use, avoid collecting from any but the most common plants.

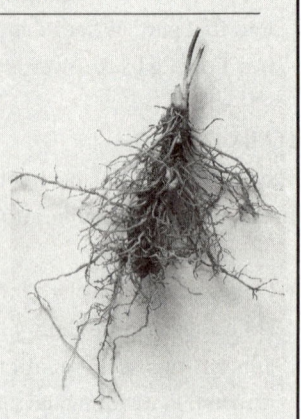

ABOVE THE RANGE OF GOLDEN SEAL HAS DIMINISHED DUE TO OVER-GATHERING.

PROCESSING YOUR HERBS

If the herbs are not to be used fresh, begin the storing process immediately. Two things are needed to preserve herbs at their best: dehydration to remove all traces of moisture; and careful storage to protect from light, damp and heat.

DRYING

Gently shake, brush or wash away any trace of dirt, dust or insects, and dry any remaining damp. Then proceed with the correct method according to which particular parts of the plant you are drying.

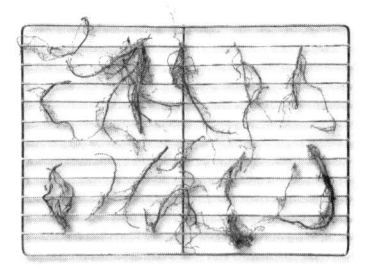

ABOVE PLACE HARVESTED ROOTS ON A RACK AND LEAVE IN A WARM, DRY PLACE UNTIL THEY ARE THOROUGHLY DRY.

Roots and Bark

Chop roots and bark into small pieces before drying to speed dehydration and make them easier to handle later. Lay pieces out on a rack or cloth away from direct light in a warm place such as the airing cupboard, the top of a boiler, or near a wood stove. To dry more quickly, place the herbs in a warm oven on the very lowest setting, warming the oven, then turning off the heat and reheating briefly and periodically to maintain the lowest temperature.

Leaves and Flowering Stems

Tie these in small bundles at the base and hang them upside down in a warm, dry, airy place, out of light, where the air can circulate freely around them. Protect them from dust by placing under a muslin cloth, or in a paper bag with holes punched in. When dry, spread out a large clean cloth or piece of paper to catch the leaves or flowers as you rub or cut them off. Light stems may be kept and chopped into small pieces.

Flowering Heads

Place flowering heads on a tray or on a cloth stretched across a frame and keep in a warm dark place. Check them frequently and turn them to speed up the drying process. When dry, the flowers may be rubbed gently to break them into smaller pieces, especially if they are to be put into mixtures.

Fruit

Either keep on the stem, hang up as for leaves and remove when dry, or remove individual fruits carefully and dry as for root pieces. Fruit peel may be stripped and chopped before drying as for roots.

Seeds

Dry the seed head whole, hanging it by the stem. When dry, lay out a large, clean sheet of paper or cloth and shake the seed heads and/or rub them over it. Alternatively, remove the seeds when first collected over the sheet, then spread them on a tray to dry in a warm place away from light.

The test for the completion of the drying process is to feel the material; it should feel crisp and dry, and crumble or break easily with a snap.

ABOVE SEEDS THAT ARE READY FOR USE FEEL CRISP AND DRY TO THE TOUCH.

Storing Your Herbs

While herbs will keep for several years in the right conditions, it is best to gather them freshly and dry them each year, especially in the case of aromatic ones. Once dried, herbs may be placed in any clean, dry container with a tight fitting lid. Identify and date the herbs with a label on the container. Store the containers away from heat and direct sunlight.

Using Your Herbs

There are many different ways of taking herbs, from simply eating them raw to brewing a delicious aromatic tea or applying them as an oil or ointment. The kitchen becomes a veritable pharmacy in itself! The therapeutic effect you desire determines the choice of preparation and whether it is applied internally or externally.

INFUSIONS

An infusion, or herbal tea, is made with the lighter, more delicate or aerial parts of a plant – such as the leaves, flowers and non-woody stems – and may be taken internally or applied externally. Medicinal-strength tea is made with one cup of water for each teaspoon of dried herbs or two teaspoons of fresh herbs. For full effect, it should be left to brew for at least 15 minutes. Be sure to use only ceramic, stainless steel or glass containers, never metals such as aluminium.

Some teas are taken cool. Make the tea by steeping the herbs cold in water overnight or through the day, especially in a sunny spot.

ABOVE TO MAKE A TEA, USE A TEASPOON OF DRIED HERBS FOR EVERY ONE CUP OF WATER. BREW FOR 15 MINUTES.

DECOCTIONS

When the medicinal properties of a plant are concentrated in its tougher parts – the inner bark, roots, rhizomes, woody stems or seeds – they are extracted by a decoction. The proportions are the same as for an infusion. Instead of brewing, however, a decoction slowly simmers in a covered pan for 15–20 minutes. Again, always use a glass, enamel or stainless steel pan, never aluminium, brass, copper, or non-stick-coated pans.

INHALATIONS

Prepare a tea with the appropriate aromatic herbs. Pour the tea into a basin, place a large towel over the head, bend over the basin, enclosing your face in the steam with the towel. Breathe calmly, inhaling the aromatic steam. At intervals, pause for ordinary breathing. Repeat four or five times or until relieved.

LEFT FOR AN INHALATION, PLACE A LARGE TOWEL OVER YOUR HEAD AND THE BASIN TO MAKE A TENT. BREATHE SLOWLY AND DEEPLY FOR AS LONG AS THE STEAM LASTS.

WASHES

Herbal teas can be used to bathe a local area of skin affected by, for example, skin eruptions, itching or inflammation. They may be used to bathe the body during a fever, and for hair rinses.

FOOT AND HAND BATHS

This method was used extensively by the French herbalist Maurice Messegue to great effect. He prescribed warm foot or hand baths for eight minutes, morning and evening. Prepare enough tea to cover the foot or hand to the ankle or wrist, as hot as is comfortable.

RIGHT A WARMING HAND BATH CAN BE A VERY EFFECTIVE TREATMENT AND IS PARTICULARLY GOOD FOR THOSE WHO DISLIKE THE TASTE OF A HERB.

TINCTURES

These are like cold infusions of herbs but instead of using water as solvent, spirits, such as brandy or vodka (60% proof), are used. The spirits act as preservatives, so the preparation will keep. They are not suitable for those who do not like, or cannot take, alcohol. Tinctures may also be made with apple-cider vinegar.

To prepare a tincture, use a clean, wide-mouth large jar with a tight-fitting lid. Chop the herbs beforehand or use powders. Combine 1pt (570ml) of vodka with 4oz (113g) of dried herb, 8oz (227g) of fresh herb, in the jar. Cap the jar tightly and place away from direct sunlight. Shake the tincture at least three times a day. Macerate (soak) the tincture in this way for two weeks, then strain away the herbs and bottle the tincture in a brown glass container. Seal with a wax-coated cork or tight cap.

ABOVE ONCE THE TINCTURE HAS BEEN MADE, BOTTLE THE LIQUID IN DARK GLASS CONTAINERS AND SEAL WITH A TIGHT-FITTING CAP.

LINIMENTS

These are made exactly like tinctures. They are for external use as muscle rubs, or for applying to cuts and wounds. Apple-cider vinegar is a good medium, as is surgical spirit. Good herbs to use are warming, penetrating and antiseptic ones such as ginger, eucalyptus, cayenne, black pepper and myrrh; or cooling, healing, astringent ones such as golden seal, marigold, St John's wort and comfrey leaf.

RIGHT MARIGOLD CAN BE USED IN A LINIMENT.

SYRUPS

Syrups are made for coughs, sore throats and respiratory conditions. Brew a strong herb tea then mix with an equal amount of honey or glycerine. Alternatively, concentrate the herbal tea by simmering it down slowly to half its original amount and then adding raw, brown sugar or honey to thicken. Herbs such as thyme, violet leaves, sage, garlic and licorice all make good syrups. Store in the refrigerator for up to a week.

POULTICES

This treatment is a local external application and used for local areas of inflammation, traumatized vertebrae, broken bones, itching, arthritis, rheumatism, bursitis, boils, psoriasis, eczema, sprained muscles and ligaments, joint aches and lower back pain. Poultices are valuable for first aid to wounds and burns, even major ones.

Cut a clean cotton cloth twice the size of the area you want to cover. Blend the selected herbs either dried, fresh (chopped small) or powdered. Include a herb such as slippery elm or a small amount of flour, cornflour (starch) or cornmeal to act as a binding agent and give bulk. Put the herbs on the cloth and place the cloth on a plate or shallow bowl. Pour on just enough boiled water to moisten and create a thick mass. Wrap the sides around the herbs, and place the poultice, warm or cool as needed, on the area to be covered. Cover with clingfilm to retain moisture and with a thick towel or blanket to retain heat. Replace as needed. Poultices may be left on overnight.

OILS AND OINTMENTS

Herbal oils can be used for salad dressings, for massage and for muscle rubs and earaches. Healing ointments are easily made from herbal oils by simply adding beeswax or cocoa butter. Aromatherapy massage oils may be made from your own garden herbs such as lavender, rosemary, thyme, St John's wort and mint. Ginger and garlic make useful oils.

To make a herbal oil, fill a wide-mouth jar with 1pt (570ml) of any good light vegetable oil, such as grapeseed, soy or sunflower, preferably cold-pressed. Add 2.5oz (70g) of dried herb or 5oz (140g) of

LEFT ST JOHN'S WORT IS COMMONLY USED TO MAKE A HERBAL MASSAGE OIL.

fresh herbs, cover tightly and macerate in a warm place for three days. Strain away the herb and bottle the oil in sterile bottles. To make a stronger oil, replace with more herbs and repeat as desired. When the oil is needed right away, warm herbs in oil gently on a low flame for an hour; strain. Store oils in a cool place.

To make a healing ointment for the first-aid kit, prepare a herbal oil as above using comfrey leaves, chickweed, calendula, plantain or yarrow. Warm the strained oil; grate in one or more ounces of beeswax or cocoa butter, stirring until melted. Test for consistency by coating a spoon; it should solidify within moments. Add more beeswax if necessary. Pour into sterilized jars and cap.

PILLS AND CAPSULES

This is a convenient, tasteless, way to take herbs that involves the least processing, so is closer to raw form. Many herbs can be powdered finely enough in a home blender.

To make pills, mix 1–2 tablespoons of honey for 1oz (28g) of herb; the amount of honey varies with the texture of the herbs. Add a small

ABOVE TO FILL THE CAPSULES, SIMPLY SCOOP UP SOME OF THE POWDERED HERB INTO EACH END OF THE OPENED CAPSULE.

amount of boiled water gradually until the powder thickens to a dough-like consistency; adding a little slippery elm powder or flour will help this. Roll the dough into a ball and pinch off small amounts; roll between your fingers to the shape and size of a pea. Flatten these between your fingers and place on a baking

LEFT EMPTY GELATINE CAPSULES CAN BE OBTAINED FROM A HEALTH-FOOD SHOP OR A CHEMIST.

tray. Warm in a very slow oven until the moisture is removed. Store the pills in an airtight jar and keep in the refrigerator. The honey will act as a preservative.

To fill capsules, obtain some gelatine capsules from a health-food shop or chemist. Place the powdered herbs in a bowl. Take each capsule and separate, then tap each end in the powder to fill before replacing the ends together.

THE HERBAL PILLOW

A herbal pillow can be used for conditions ranging from pre-menstrual tension to asthma. They are especially good for children.

Choose the dried herbs for your condition. Cut a small muslin cloth about nine inches square. Place the herbs inside and sew it up. Place the pillow inside your pillow case and the healing energies will do their work while you sleep. Renew the pillow at least annually.

Dosages

The effects of herbs depend to an extent on how often they are taken. For acute ailments, it is generally best to take the herbs quite frequently, every hour or even half hour, until the symptoms start to subside. Then continue the dose at gradually longer intervals up to two or three times a day until the condition clears.

HERB TEAS AND DECOCTIONS

Adults should take one cup every hour or so to relieve symptoms for short-term, acute conditions, then one cup three times a day for follow-up or longer-term treatment.

CAPSULES OR PILLS

Adults should take two capsules or four pills every hour as needed in acute conditions, or three times a day with meals for follow-up and longer-term treatment.

TINCTURES

Adults take 1tsp (5ml) every hour as needed, or three times a day for follow-up or longer-term treatment.

POULTICES OR EXTERNAL APPLICATIONS

Judge according to the situation, and use the same general guideline – apply frequently until relieved, then less often.

LONG-TERM IMBALANCES

For imbalances that have been present for some time, but are not manifesting acutely at the moment, the dosage should be one cup, 1tsp or two capsules three times a day for three weeks. Rest one week, then re-assess, and repeat if needed.

CHILDREN

For children, the adult dose is reduced proportionately according to age; this is based on weight, so make adjustments if the child is not average weight for age. Dilute with water or juice.

- Nursing infants: The mother should take the herbs – their effects will pass through the milk to the baby.
- 6mth–1 year: ⅛ or less (depending on weight) of adult dose
- 1–2 years: ¼ of adult dose
- 3–7 years: ½ of adult dose
- 7–12 years: ¾ of adult dose

RIGHT CHILDREN AGED BETWEEN THREE AND SEVEN SHOULD TAKE HALF THE ADULT DOSAGE.

ELDERLY

For elderly patients, adjust the dose according to how frail they are. If they are hardy and sturdy, even if old, the adult dose can apply. If frail and weak, use the doses for small children under seven.

> ### How Many Herbs to Use?
>
> For short-term, one-off ailments, a single herb can be very effective, provided it is taken strongly and often enough. Such a herb is called a simple.
>
> A good example of simpling is taking echinacea at the first sign of a cold or flu, or eating raw garlic paste or drinking copious amounts of elderflower tea. This will either prevent the condition worsening altogether or lighten its course; nothing further needs to be done except to continue with the one herb for a few days extra to thoroughly clear the condition. Try several simples to find the one that best suits you.
>
> For other ailments that have perhaps happened regularly before or have been around vaguely for a while before they manifest strongly, it is better to use herbs in blends or formulas. The amounts of the different herbs included are important and there are some general guidelines for this.
>
> The greater part of a herbal blend should be given to the herb that most directly affects the condition. For example, in a fever this would be the cooling, antipyretic, blood-purifying herb. This herb can then be reinforced by including the same amount of another herb or two with the same main action. Such a herb should also have a secondary action different from that of the main herb but that complements or extends the main action. These three or four herbs are often enough for simple conditions.
>
> If you feel your ailment involves some greater imbalance, weakness or excess, then a more complex blend may be called for.

In this case, again choose two or three main but complementary herbs. Then, consider which additional aspect of the body needs support and choose one or two other herbs that extend the action of the blend to this area. For example, in the case of a Water person who has a cold, it would be suggested that laxative and diuretic herbs be added to help clear any residual stagnation in the system.

Finally, it is a good rule to include both a circulation-stimulating herb, either mild or strong depending on the individual, which will help to carry the action of the other herbs through to the tissues efficiently, and a relaxing herb that will relieve residual tension and allow the tissues to be more receptive to the herbal effects. These can be added at one half the amount of the main herb.

ABOVE DRINKING ELDERFLOWER TEA AT THE FIRST SIGN OF A COLD OR FLU WILL OFTEN ALLEVIATE SYMPTOMS AND NEGATE THE NECESSITY OF TAKING FURTHER MEDICATION.

MATERIA MEDICA

CHAPTER SIX

Materia medica means the materials of medicine, a listing of herbs with a description of their characteristics, parts used and properties. The selection presented here is necessarily limited, but tries to include herbs that are easy to find commercially, in gardens or in the wild, as well as four extremely useful oriental herbs.

ALOE VERA
Aloe vera (A. barbadensis)
Part used: flesh of leaf stems.
Properties: blood purifier, antiseptic, antipyretic, purgative, laxative.
Energy: cooling, moistening. Reduces Fire, clears stagnant water, calms Air.
Caution: do not use aloe internally in the presence of internal bleeding or heavy menstruation.

ABOVE ALOE VERA HAS LONG, SUCCULENT, DARK GREEN LEAVES.

LEFT TO OBTAIN THE SOOTHING ALOE GEL, SIMPLY CUT A LEAF INTO PIECES.

Aloe vera deserves a place in every garden or home. In colder climates, it thrives as a house plant. It is the first-aid plant par excellence: one only has to pinch off a bit of the fleshy leaves and peel back the outer skin to obtain the cooling antiseptic and healing properties of the clear gel. Use for acne, skin complaints, burns and wounds. Take internally, 1tsp diluted with water, for blood cleansing and as a bowel cleanser.

BASIL
Ocimum basilicum
Parts used: leaves, flowering stem.
Properties: energy stimulant, respiratory decongestant, carminative, diaphoretic, nervine. Uplifts and clears the mind and head.
Energy: warming, clearing, dispersing. Increases Fire, reduces excess Water, calms Air.
Caution: avoid prolonged concentrated use during first trimester of pregnancy. Safe for occasional tea, culinary and short-term uses.

The Indian species of basil holds a high place in Ayurvedic medicine. It is planted around the doors of houses for its purifying effect both on the physical and the emotional and mental levels. All basils reduce excess mucous and improve digestion. They have a refreshing, uplifting and purifying quality. They are easy-to-grow annuals that should be used regularly in cooking as well as for medicine.

BAYBERRY
Myrica pennsylvanica
Part used: bark.
Properties: stimulant, aromatic. Clears excess mucous (Water), diaphoretic, expectorant, astringent
Energy: warming, stimulating, increases Fire, reduces excess Water, calms Air.

Bayberry is a North American herb highly valued for its stimulating properties. Bayberry is most used today for conditions of excess mucous such as colds and sinus congestion, and even mucous in the intestines and bowel inflammation.

BURDOCK

Arctium lappa

Part used: root.
Properties: blood purifier, tonic, diuretic, diaphoretic, astringent.
Energy: cool, drying. Reduces Fire, reduces excess Water, increases Air mildly.

BELOW BURDOCK HAS LARGE WAVY LEAVES AND IS FOUND GROWING ON WAYSIDES.

Burdock is one of those valuable weeds of fields and waysides. It cleanses the blood through its action on both the liver and the kidneys. Overburdened blood is a major factor behind arthritis, fevers, infections and skin conditions such as boils and sores. Being a starchy root, it also supplies nutrition and builds strong blood with its iron content. Yellow dock, although not related botanically, has similar properties.

CALAMUS, SWEET

Acorus calamus

Part used: root.
Properties: nutritive tonic, nervine and brain tonic, digestive aid, clears mucous. Circulating and invigorating.
Energy: warming, calming. Reduces excess Water. Calms and strengthens Air. Mildly increases Fire.
Caution: Use short term only.

BELOW THE DRIED ROOT OF THE SWEET CALAMUS IS USED IN HERBAL MEDICINE.

Sweet calamus grows naturally near ponds and waterways. It holds a high place in Ayurvedic medicine as being purifying to the body and the mind and promoting longevity with its rejuvenating qualities. It tonifies digestion, thereby clearing the blood and lymph, and strengthens the nerves. Like comfrey, it is a starchy root with nutritive qualities.

Used externally as a locally applied paste, it calms headaches and pain. In the US it is currently listed as not recommended by the Food and Drugs Administration (FDA) for internal use, though it is used thus routinely in India and in the UK.

CATNIP

Nepeta cataria
Parts used: leaves, flowering stem.
Properties: nervine, reduces fever, gently carminative, diaphoretic, stomachic.
Energy: cooling and balancing.

Catnip is especially good for children and the elderly, as its action is gently stimulating and clearing while still being effective. It is best combined with fennel for digestive and calming effects.

ABOVE THE LEAVES AND FLOWERING TOPS OF CATNIP ARE GATHERED IN THE SUMMER FOR USE IN HERBAL REMEDIES.

CAYENNE

Capsicum annuum var. annuum
Part used: fruit.
Properties: heating, stimulating, blood regulator/haemostatic, diaphoretic, anti-infectious, astringent, carminative, antispasmodic.
Energy: hot, stimulating. Increases Fire but can also disperse excess heat
Caution: avoid concentrated prolonged use in pregnancy, hypertension and peptic ulcers.

ABOVE CAYENNE POWDER HAS WARMING AND STIMULATING PROPERTIES AND CAN HELP TO INCREASE CIRCULATION TO STIFF JOINTS.

Cayenne is an excellent herb to have on hand for emergencies. It counters shock and can arrest bleeding by its astringency and ability to penetrate tissue quickly and to normalize blood flow – that is, to channel blood away from the site of bleeding, whether internal or external (see Herbs for First Aid, p.119). Its warmth improves circulation to stiff joints. It benefits digestion and is powerful for clearing excess mucous from the stomach. It has been used to heal stomach ulcers. It normalizes both high and low blood pressure. Cayenne is often an ingredient in formulas for its ability to carry the other herbs quickly where they are needed. It can be taken on a daily basis of ¼–1tsp taken at breakfast mixed with juice, water or yoghurt. Chillies are used similarly.

CHAMOMILE

Chamaemelum nobile and *Matricaria recutita*

Part used: flowering heads.

Properties: carminative, aromatic, diaphoretic, nervine. Roman Chamomile (*Chamaemelum nobile*) is more anti-inflammatory, German chamomile (*Matricaria recutita*) is more antispasmodic.

Energy: cooling, calming. Reduces excess Water, cools Fire, stabilizes Air.

ABOVE GERMAN CHAMOMILE HAS DELICATE APPLE-SCENTED DAISY-LIKE FLOWERS. IT IS USED HERBALLY AS A SEDATIVE.

For those who enjoy its soft apple-like flavour, chamomile is a good all-purpose remedy. It helps induce calmness and sound sleep. It clears digestive upsets. It helps clear mucous build-up, so can be used for colds, fever and flu. It is perhaps ideal for Fire types who, through stress, anger and overwork get digestive upsets, sleep poorly or come down with a bad cold.

The flavour is often attractive to children, making it an excellent choice when treating them for complaints such as poor sleep, upset stomach or colds.

CHICKWEED

Stellaria media

Parts used: leaves and flowering stems.
Properties: demulcent, astringent, diuretic, vulnerary.
Energy: cooling, reduces excess Water, cools Fire, mildly increases Air.

BELOW CHICKWEED GROWS PROLIFICALLY IN GARDENS AND FIELDS. IT IS A GOOD REMEDY FOR CUTS AND SKIN IRRITATIONS.

Although considered an invasive weed, this plant should be allowed a corner in every garden. It can be eaten as a pot-herb in salads. It is excellent as a mild diuretic, stimulating to the kidneys, reducing weight and water. Used in ointments or as a bath tea, it is beneficial for wounds and skin complaints such as itching, redness and inflammation.

CLEAVERS

Galium aparine

Parts used: leaves and flowering stems.
Properties: diuretic, blood purifying, laxative.
Energy: cooling, drying. Reduces Water, cools Fire, mildly increases Air.

Cleavers are those prolific garden weeds that have a strange dry, sticky texture so that they cling when pressed against the body. Children enjoy playing with them for this reason. This herb has similar uses to chickweed but is a stronger diuretic. As well as benefitting skin problems and fevers, it finds a place in weight-reduction formulas and to treat oedema and clear kidney stones.

CLOVE

Eugenia caryophyllus
Part used: flowering bud.
Properties: nervine – anaesthetic, analgesic – aromatic, digestive and circulatory stimulant, carminative, expectorant.
Energy: warming, stimulating. Reduces excess water (mucous, damp), increases Fire, calms Air.

Cloves are used mainly to improve digestive upsets and to clear excess mucous in the lungs, for example in asthma, coughs or colds. As warming carminatives, they improve digestion and assimilation of foods and can so raise energy levels and lower blood pressure. Their nervine-analgesic, even numbing, properties provide relief for toothaches and other pain.

COLTSFOOT

Tussilago faifara
Parts used: leaves, flowers.
Properties: demulcent, expectorant, astringent.
Energy: cooling, dispersing.

Coltsfoot's name describes the hoof-like shape of its leaves. It grows easily in damp waste places and will grow quickly in the garden, so plant it in a container or out-of-the-way spot. It appears very early in spring, when its dandelion-like flowers come before the leaves. Coltsfoot is a tried and true remedy for coughs, helping to liquefy mucous, cool irritated passages and expel the phlegm. It will also relieve diarrhoea because of its astringent action. Crushed leaves make a good poultice for stings and bites.

ABOVE DRIED COLTSFOOT FLOWERS CAN BE USED IN HERBAL REMEDIES. THEIR EXPECTORANT PROPERTIES HELP CHEST AND LUNG PROBLEMS.

COMFREY
Symphytum officinalis
Parts used: leaves and flowers. Root under direction of herbalist.
Properties: tonic, demulcent, blood regulator – arrests bleeding and builds blood; vulnerary (tissue healing). Especially good for respiratory system, weakness and anaemia, muscular system.
Energy: cooling, nutritive tonic. Strengthens Water essence and vital fluids. Cools Fire.

There has been a lot of controversy over comfrey, as claims have been made, based on flawed research, that it is carcinogenic. Yet comfrey is an invaluable herb. It especially benefits the lungs, is soothing to coughs and bronchial inflammation. The starchy root is used as a nutritive tonic and renewer of tissue in wasting diseases. It can stop bleeding and heal external and internal tissues. So it is beneficial where bleeding occurs from ulcers, lungs, kidneys or bowels. Comfrey is a tremendous healer of minor or severe burns and wounds, soothing the trauma and promoting growth of new, healthy tissue.

CRAMP BARK
Viburnum opulus
Part used: inner bark of limbs.
Properties: antispasmodic, nervine, astringent.
Energy: warming, relaxing. Calms Air.

ABOVE CRAMP BARK, AS ITS NAME SUGGESTS, IS USED TO RELIEVE CRAMP.

Cramp bark and its relative black haw (*Viburnum prunifolium*) are valued for their effects on menstrual cramps, especially when combined with ginger. The warmth circulates energy in the pelvic region, relieving blood congestion; the antispasmodic action relaxes excessive uterine contractions; the astringency tones the tissues. Its nervine action is general and also benefits heart palpitations and asthma.

CUMIN

Cuminum cyminum
Part used: seeds.
Properties: carminative, digestive aid, antispasmodic, stimulant, alterative.
Energy: warming and cooling. Reduces excess Fire and Water. Calms Air.

BELOW USE CUMIN WITH FOODS SUCH AS TOMATOES TO COUNTERACT THEIR HEATING EFFECTS.

Cumin is one of the culinary spices that is useful for many medicinal purposes. It alleviates gas and indigestion, colic and diarrhoea. Fire types especially should use it regularly, particularly with heating foods such as tomatoes or hot spices as it counteracts their heating effects. Cumin improves the assimilation of foods.

DANDELION

Taraxacum officinalis
Parts used: leaves and root.
Properties: diuretic, blood purifier, liver tonic, stomachic, nutritive.
Energy: cooling. Reduces excess Water (damp), cools Fire, stabilizes Air.

Dandelion is a very important herb, finding a place in the treatment of both acute and chronic illnesses. Herbalists use it as part of treatment for diabetes, kidney and gall bladder obstructions, heart disease and liver disease such as hepatitis. Both the leaves and the root are nutritive, providing valuable minerals; the root is stronger and preferred for medicinal use, though the leaves are also valuable. It is an excellent blood purifier through its action both on the liver and the kidneys, as its French name *pis en lit* (wet the bed) tells us. It can be used for acute stomach aches in the form of a decoction and to help reduce excess weight. Regular use from time to time keeps the internal organs clear and healthy. Chopping, roasting, then powdering the dried root makes an excellent coffee substitute.

ECHINACEA

Echinacea angustifolia and E. purpurea
Part used: root.
Properties: antibiotic, immune tonic, blood and lymph purifier, fever reducing.
Energy: cooling, tonifying, dispersing. Reduces Fire and Water, increases Air.

Echinacea has grown in importance only relatively recently. A native of the plains region of the western United States, it was used by Native Americans. Recent research has confirmed it as a powerful natural antibiotic. It not only kills bacteria and viruses but actually strengthens immunity by increasing the number of white blood cells in the bloodstream. It can be used as a safe alternative to synthetic antibiotics. Echinacea is most conveniently taken in powder or tincture form, two capsules or 1tsp every hour at the first sign of a cold, flu or fever or whenever antibiotic action is needed. Discontinue after ten days. It is also effective against vaginal yeast infections, candida, urinary tract and skin infections.

ABOVE ECHINACEA TINCTURE HAS GOOD ANTIVIRAL PROPERTIES.

ELDERFLOWER

Sambucus nigra
Parts used: berries, leaves, flowers.
Properties: diaphoretic, expectorant, diuretic.
Energy: cooling, dispersing. Reduces Fire and Water, stabilizes Air.

Several parts of the elder tree give relief in many conditions. The fragrant flowers make an excellent

ABOVE ELDERBERRY CORDIAL MAKES A DELICIOUS COOLING DRINK FOR SUMMER.

diaphoretic tea for use in colds, flu and fevers. Their action is enhanced when combined with peppermint or ginger and lemon. They make a delicious cordial, mixed with citrus lemon, lime or orange, which can be drunk hot in the winter or cool in summer. The ripe berries make an excellent cough syrup and the leaves can be made into an ointment for skin complaints.

FENNEL
Foeniculum vulgare
Part used: seeds.
Properties: diuretic, demulcent, carminative.
Energy: warming, softening, moistening, balancing. Increases digestive Fire while reducing excess Fire, reduces Water, stabilizes Air. Balances all three humours.
Caution: avoid prolonged or concentrated use during first trimester of pregnancy. Safe for occasional tea, culinary and short-term uses.

Fennel is an easily available culinary herb with good medicinal value. It improves digestion and thus helps clear toxic accumulations from the system. It is diuretic and helps remove excess damp and fat from the system. For gas, cramp or colitis upsets, combine it with catnip, licorice or anise. Fennel tea can be used externally to calm any skin inflammation. The seeds should be decocted or powdered before infusing. Fennel can be used by all three constitutional types.

GARLIC
Allium sativum
Part used: corms.
Properties: circulatory stimulant, antiseptic, blood purifier, diaphoretic, digestive stimulant, carminative, expectorant, tonic.
Energy: warming, stimulating, sweet. Reduces Water and grounds excessive Air, increases digestive Fire.
Caution: avoid prolonged concentrated use during first trimester of pregnancy. Safe for occasional tea, culinary and short-term uses.

Garlic should be found in every home. Used regularly, it is an overall tonic for the system, helping to promote good digestion and assimilation, and strengthening the adrenal glands. It stimulates and improves blood circulation, because it clears cholesterol and other impurities from the blood. It therefore finds a place in treating excess weight, lymphatic congestion, hypertension and heart disease. However, it should be avoided in any bleeding conditions, such as excessive menstrual bleeding or blood in the stools.

Garlic is a natural antibiotic. Eating a clove raw or expressing the juice into one tablespoon of vegetable oil at the first sign of a cold, flu or any infection will usually clear or at least weaken it. Good quality garlic powder can be used instead of raw garlic, though it will not be quite as effective.

GINGER
Zingiber officinalis
Part used: rhizome.
Properties: circulatory stimulant, antispasmodic, antiseptic, diaphoretic, expectorant, carminative, analgesic.
Energy: warming, slightly drying, relaxing. Reduces excess Water (mucous); stimulates digestive Fire. Clears excess Fire and calms Air.

This common culinary spice is a virtual treasure trove because it benefits such a wide variety of conditions. Its aroma instantly calms and purifies. Both powder and fresh ginger are used, but powdered ginger is hotter and more drying than fresh.

An instant massage oil can be made by grating the fresh root and mixing the juice with a little vegetable oil. This will ease the stiffness and pain of arthritis or any cramping or muscular tension. A small piece used regularly in cooking improves the digestibility of foods, especially meats, and thus helps maintain health.

By combining ginger powder with a little water and flour, a paste is created for an external application for headaches or pain anywhere.

As an antispasmodic, ginger finds a place in treating intestinal or menstrual cramps and tension generally. A little ginger can be added to almost any herbal combination to ensure circulation and good penetration to tissues. It blends well with other diaphoretics to treat colds, flu and fevers. It relieves stomach upsets, belching, gas and nausea, particularly nausea during pregnancy or while travelling. It helps clear stagnant mucous congestion in the lung area. To improve its action, Water types should mix it with honey, Fire types with dark, raw sugar and Air types with salt.

GOLDEN SEAL
Hydrastis canadensis
Part used: root.
Properties: antibiotic, blood purifying, antipyretic, bitter stomach tonic, astringent, emmenagogue, laxative.
Energy: cooling and drying. Lowers high Fire, cleanses congested Water (mucous), increases Air.
Caution: This herb is not suitable for prolonged use due to a possible tendency to imbalance intestinal flora. It is best avoided during the first trimester of pregnancy because its effect on the uterus may increase the chance of a miscarriage.

This Appalachian wild flower is literally worth its weight in gold, as its name suggests. It is fairly expensive to purchase but well worth it as it so efficiently deals with so many problems and a small amount of the herb goes a long way.

Golden seal is particularly effective at protecting mucous membranes – the thin layers of protection that line much of the body including the entire respiratory, digestive, urinary and reproductive tracts. Golden seal can also treat inflammation and infection.

Golden seal deals with such ailments as colds and flu, respiratory catarrh; infections, inflammation in the stomach and intestines (ulcers, nausea, colitis, irritable bowel, gastroenteritis); vaginal and urinary tract infections, skin eruptions, boils and infections in wounds. At the same time as healing the symptoms in these organs and tissues, golden seal tones and improves their function for the future. Its bitter properties purge and strengthen the stomach, liver and bowels. Golden seal combines well with echinacea for a natural and effective antibiotic.

Because of its astringent properties, golden seal should be avoided in the first three months of pregnancy as its contracting effect on the uterus may contribute to a miscarriage.

HAWTHORN

Crataegus oxycantha (C. laevigata)
Parts used: berries, flowers may be used but are milder.
Properties: heart tonic, circulatory stimulant and regulator, antispasmodic, astringent.
Energy: warm. Decreases excess Air while stimulating Fire.

BELOW THE FLOWERING HAWTHORN FLOWERS ARE DRIED AND USED IN HERBAL MEDICINE.

Hawthorn is probably one of the most abundant herbs still growing wild in the UK. Both flowers and berries used to be eaten by country folk.

There is a strong tradition in British herbal medicine for using hawthorn as a heart remedy. Hawthorn increases coronary circulation. It strengthens the heart muscle cells, nourishes them and increases energy, without over-stimulating. It increases the force of the beat but not the rate. Hawthorn also evens irregular and arrhythmic heartbeat. It has antispasmodic and nervine qualities. Its most obvious use is as part of the treatment for hypertension and tachycardia. It is safe to use with elderly people who are beginning to experience loss of function. Those passing from middle to older age should consider using it on a regular, periodic basis as part of tonification and rejuvenation therapy.

HOPS

Humulus lupulus
Part used: flowers.
Properties: nervine (calming, sleep-inducing), bitter digestive, tonic, pain-relieving.
Energy: cooling. Decreases excited Air while strengthening digestive Fire to enhance the digestion and assimilation of food energy. Coolness will aggravate Air in the long term, so Air types should be sure to combine it with a warming herb for balanced effect.

Hop flowers are a well-known ingredient in both beers and herbal pillows. The belief that ales and stouts will strengthen weak individuals is explained by the bitter principles in hops, which act to stimulate the digestive enzymes and therefore increase nutrition. The nervine properties enhance sleep, which gives the body time to rest and repair, so hops are often found in herbal pillows. Recent studies show a hormone-regulating action, which improves reproductive function in both men and women. For sleeplessness, simply brew a tea before bedtime or make a herbal pillow. For sleep, combine hops with lime flowers or chamomile. Externally, a hop poultice or wash will cool and relieve pain and inflammation.

HORSETAIL

Equisetum arvense
Parts used: stem and leaves.
Properties: astringent, diuretic, diaphoretic, blood purifying.
Energy: cooling, drying. Removes excess Water (damp), lowers and purges excess Fire from the blood. Increases Air so prolonged use in those tending to dryness is not recommended.

ABOVE HORSETAIL HAS NO LEAVES BUT WHORLS OF SMALL GREEN BRANCHES.

This plant looks rather like a horse's tail, with its bony stem and hair-like leaves. It is one of the most ancient plants, dating back to the age of dinosaurs.

Horsetail grows in damp places. Traditional medicine holds that plants in such habitats are often the most effective for treating problems of fluid retention – they drain the damp collecting in the body. Horsetail is primarily a diuretic and is used for lymphatic congestion, bladder infections, cystitis and kidney stones. It also acts to cleanse the liver and gall bladder and its diaphoretic action is useful to lower fevers as in flu or infections. Horsetail is high in silica, which helps break up calcium deposited in tissues (urinary stones, or around joints). It is also high in calcium, which nourishes bones and nerve tissue.

HYSSOP

Hyssopus officinalis
Part used: flowering stem.
Properties: aromatic, diaphoretic, anti-infectious, circulatory stimulant, expectorant, nervine.
Energy: warming, drying. Reduces excess or stagnant Water (phlegm, mucous); mildly increases Fire; calms and regulates Air.

Hyssop is a cleansing herb, especially of the respiratory tract. Like all aromatic plants, it is a powerful germicide and was once used to deter insects and vermin from homes and skin. Its mucous-clearing and nervine properties give it a place in treating bronchial congestion and even asthma. By releasing stagnation, it promotes the smooth flow of Vital Energy, especially that derived from Air.

ABOVE HYSSOP IS A HARDY SHRUB WITH PURPLE FLOWERS.

JUNIPER

Juniperus communis
Parts used: berries, stem.
Properties: diuretic, carminative, diaphoretic, blood-purifying, anti-infectious, tonic.
Energy: warming, drying. Reduces excess Water, purges excess Fire and stimulates digestive Fire; warming to Air types at the same time it clears excess Air humour.
Caution: Do not use in cases of nephritis (chronic kidney inflammation). Avoid prolonged concentrated use during first trimester of pregnancy.

ABOVE JUNIPER IS A LOW PRICKLY EVERGREEN BUSH. IT HAS SILVERY-GREEN SPINY NEEDLES.

Juniper berries are a common culinary flavouring. They are also used in the distillation of gin. Juniper's primary areas of action are on the digestive and urinary systems. Its warm, aromatic qualities aid digestion. It both stimulates the diuretic action of the kidneys and warms the circulation, helping to eliminate excess damp and cold. It also strengthens the adrenal glands. It finds a place in treating water retention, lymphatic congestion, arthritis, gout, rheumatism, stones, cystitis and bladder infections.

KELP

Fucus vesiculosis
Part used: leaves.
Properties: tonic, nourishing, demulcent, expectorant, diuretic. High in minerals and vitamins; a natural supplement.
Energy: cooling and moistening. Tonifies bodily fluids.
Caution: avoid self-medication in conditions of hyperthyroidism, heart and kidney disease, lung abscesses and TB.

Kelp and other seaweeds are the great gifts from the sea. Kelp carries all the positive qualities of the sea, strengthening the fluid base of the body, the water from which life springs and in which it thrives. The iodine in kelp nourishes the thyroid gland and so maintains good metabolism and glandular function. Its moistening qualities help it to dissolve and remove stagnations such as tumours and cysts, and catarrh in the respiratory tract in the form of a sore throat or cough. While strengthening the fluids, kelp's diuretic action helps drain water or excess damp. It illustrates the regulating and balancing effect herbs have on the body in general. Take kelp tablets as a daily supplement. When you want to use kelp medicinally, simply grind the tablets to a powder to blend with other herbs.

LEMON BALM
Melissa officinalis
Parts used: leaves, flowering stem.
Properties: diaphoretic, stimulant, carminative, antiseptic, circulates energy. Blood purifier, uterine tonic and blood regulator.
Energy: cooling and balancing. Calms Air, reduces Fire, clears stagnant Water and clarifies the mind.

This herb's name says it all: the uplifting, purifying zest of lemon and a balm to troubles, whether those of a depressed mind, an upset stomach or an insect-bitten skin. Its Latin name, *Melissa* – from the Greek for honey – tells us it is loved by bees, who always seem to know the best healing plants in any vicinity. Lemon balm may be particularly useful for women, to ease cramps and pre-menstrual congestion and depression.

LICORICE
Glycyrrhiza glabra
Part used: root.
Properties: demulcent, expectorant, digestive, mild laxative, tonic, nourishing, harmonizing.

Energy: neutral, moistening. Harmonizing. Strengthens vital body fluids (Water). Reduces excess damp and phlegm. Strengthens digestive Fire while lowering inflammation, calms Air.
Caution: avoid in conditions of water retention, oedema, cardiovascular disease.

Known in Chinese medicine as the Peacemaker, licorice holds a special place in herbal medicine; it has a smoothing, soothing effect and delicious flavour. It can be added to blends to harmonize the energies of the other herbs and buffer their effects. With its sweet, nutritive qualities, it benefits weakness and hypoglycaemia. It promotes hormone balance and is good for women at times such as puberty, pregnancy and menopause. Its demulcent, expectorant properties and appealing taste give it a prime place in treating coughs and congestion in the respiratory tract, especially in children. It can be made into a cough syrup, or used as a decoction. Coming from the rhizome of the plant, licorice imparts an earthy grounding quality when the Air humour is upset or imbalanced, for example in cramps or spasm. However, it should not be used by those suffering from hypertension with fluid retention or oedema.

MARIGOLD
Calendula officinalis
Part used: flowers.
Properties: anti-inflammatory, blood purifying, diaphoretic, astringent, healing.
Energy: cooling, soothing. Counters excess Fire, as in inflammation, and calms irritated Air (itching).

Marigolds are among the most charming of flowers and should be in every garden; they quickly seed themselves and will grace your home year after year. Their very shape and colour capture and reflect the optimism and brightness of the sun and summer.

Marigold is used to quell excess fire in the form of inflammation. It soothes skin abrasions, burns, stings and bites. Keep a pot of calendula ointment in your first-aid kit to soothe and promote the mending of tissue. Marigold tea is used for circulating energy and blood to dispel bruising, to regulate menses, as a diaphoretic to clear the heat of fevers and eruptive skin complaints. It combines well with comfrey or chickweed in oils or ointments.

MARSHMALLOW
Malva species
Parts used: root, leaves.
Properties: demulcent, anti-inflammatory, mucilage, blood purifying, astringent.
Energy: cooling and moistening. Increases Water, reduces Fire and Air. Strengthens vital fluids and lubricates tissue.

Just touching the leaves and flowers of marshmallow gives a clue to its qualities; they are soft and slightly thicker than most. Marshmallow, like slippery elm and comfrey, contains an abundance of mucilage that, when combined with water, swells to form a soft spongy mass. When any tissue in the body is inflamed or irritated, reach for marshmallow root. It is used for the pain and irritation of kidney stones combined with diuretics, irritable bowel or colitis combined with laxatives, and for the bronchial passages combined with expectorants.

Marshmallow root is nourishing and can be used as a nutritional supplement in weakness and convalescence.

ABOVE MARSHMALLOW HAS PINKISH WHITE BLOOMS THAT APPEAR IN LATE SUMMER TO EARLY AUTUMN.

MEADOWSWEET

Filipendula ulmaria

Parts used: flowers and leaves.
Properties: nervine (analgesic, antispasmodic), astringent, diaphoretic, diuretic.
Energy: cooling, drying. Reduces excess Water, calms aggravated Air, cools Fire.

This beautiful wayside herb with its clusters of soft, creamy and sweet smelling flowers and red-based stems, is a good source of natural aspirin. It contains salicylic compounds, from which aspirin was originally synthesized. It can be used as a natural anti-inflammatory and analgesic for headaches and acid stomach, for arthritic and rheumatic pains and urinary infections. Its other properties help dry excess damp in the system, which often lies behind these conditions.

ABOVE MEADOWSWEET HAS CLUSTERS OF CREAM-COLOURED, ALMOND-SCENTED FLOWERS.

MINTS

Mentha species

Parts used: leaves, flowering stem.
Properties: carminative, stimulating, circulates energy, diaphoretic, liver-cleansing, mucous-reducing.
Energy: warming and cooling, drying with prolonged use. Balancing. Reduces Water, cools excess Fire but promotes digestion. Calms Air.
Caution: avoid prolonged concentrated use during first trimester of pregnancy. Safe for occasional tea, culinary and short-term uses.

ABOVE PEPPERMINT HAS OVAL, POINTED AROMATIC DARK GREEN LEAVES.

The mints form a large group within the *Labatiae* family and the majority of them are excellent medicinals. Their stimulating quality is unusual in being both energizing and calming at the same time. Their action is gentle yet still very effective for the stomach, liver, nerves, blood and lymph circulation. They grow easily in gardens or on windowsills and should find a place in every home.

Peppermint (*Mentha piperita*) is the most strongly stimulating of the mints. It is actually a hybrid between pennyroyal (*M. pulegium*) and spearmint (*M. spicata*) and is sterile. It is excellent combined with elderflower for the first sign of cold or flu, or fever. As a digestive aid, it helps soothe digestion-related headaches. Many find it an acceptable substitute for coffee, giving that extra pick-up without the harmful side-effects. Its initial pungency stimulates the metabolism and is followed by a mild coolness that refreshes, making its overall action balancing to all three humours. Excessive use however, may eventually dry and aggravate Air. Spearmint is very similar to peppermint, though milder, and horsemint (*M. arvensis*) is also used.

MULLEIN
Verbascum thapsus

RIGHT MULLEIN HAS BRIGHT YELLOW FLOWERS THAT APPEAR IN MID-SUMMER.

Parts used: leaves, flowers.
Properties: demulcent, astringent, diuretic, nervine.
Energy: cooling and drying. Reduces excess Water, calms and nourishes excited Air, cools Fire.

Mullein is a visually striking plant with its tall stem rising straight and breaking out into yellow blooms at the end. The leaves too are unusual: soft, broad and fuzzy, roseate in form. Mulleins are often seen standing along highways like sentinels.

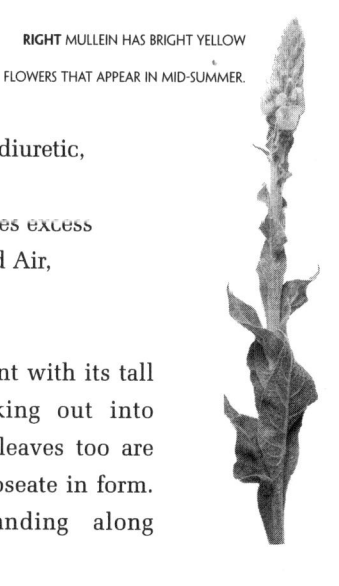

Mullein is primarily used for treating inflammations and swellings, especially when lymph nodes in the throat, neck, arms and groin swell or are congested as in sore throats, mumps and fluid in the ear. It cleanses the lymphatic system generally. For this it is applied as a poultice and taken as a tea. Its mucous-reducing properties make it useful for coughs and catarrh. It also has nervine-anodyne properties that relieve pain and promote sound sleep. Mullein tea will arrest diarrhoea.

For earache, make a herbal oil with mullein, soak a piece of cotton wool in it and place it in the ear. For Air types or for excited Air humour, infuse mullein with hot milk and drink at night before sleeping.

NETTLE

Urtica urens

Parts used: leaves and stem.

Properties: blood-purifying, circulatory stimulant, nourishing, tonic, astringent, blood-regulating (haemostatic).

Energy: cooling. Cools excess Fire while strengthening circulation. Reduces excess Water. Calms and nourishes Air.

Beyond those nasty stinging hairs lies a veritable botanical treasure. Nettle is a blood cleanser and circulatory stimulant, rich in iron and other minerals. The tender young leaves may be steamed like spinach as a pot-herb. Nettle finds a place in regulating and strengthening the blood generally, for anaemia and bleeding. It clears excess damp and so helps with arthritis and rheumatism, and with asthma and lung congestion. Its astringency and haemostatic properties signal it for diarrhoea, dysentery and excess menstrual flow. Taken regularly as a tonic tea, it helps maintain health.

ABOVE THE COMMON STINGING NETTLE IS FOUND GROWING ALL OVER THE WORLD.

OREGON GRAPE
Mahonia aquifolium
Part used: root.
Properties: blood purifying, tonifying (liver), laxative, antiseptic.
Energy: cooling. Reduces excess Fire, reduces excess Water, regulates and stabilizes Air.
Caution: Avoid prolonged concentrated use during first trimester of pregnancy. Safe for occasional tea, culinary and short-term uses.

Many gardens in Britain display this North American import, known as the holly-leafed barberry, without its owners appreciating its outstanding qualities as a liver cleanser and tonifier, blood purifier, laxative and bowel cleanser. Its Eurasian cousin, the common barberry (*Berberis vulgaris*), a shrub found in hedgerows and waysides, is used similarly, though its action is milder. The berries were once commonly eaten and prepared as condiments.

The bitter taste stimulates gastric juices, improving the digestion and assimilation of food, and purges the liver. Oregon grape and barberry are used for cases of hepatitis, jaundice, constipation, diabetes and arthritis. It is also used in problems caused by congestion of vital energy, such as moodiness or irritability in pre-menstrual tension or depression. It may be combined with turmeric for this purpose.

PARSLEY
Petroselinum crispum
Parts used: leaves, root.
Properties: diuretic, tonic, carminative, nutritive, emmenagogue.
Energy: warming, stimulating. Reduces excess

ABOVE PARSLEY CAN BE USED AS A DIGESTIVE AID AND AS A GENERAL HEALTH TONIC.

Water, and calms Air. Aggravates excess Fire when used in excess.
Caution: Avoid prolonged concentrated use during first trimester of pregnancy. Safe for occasional tea, culinary and short-term uses.

Most people don't realize how healing parsley is. The root is stronger than the leaves and better for more severe conditions. Parsley improves digestion and assimilation of food. It is an excellent diuretic and will help the body expel stones. It eases menstrual cramp, headache and tension. It supplies valuable minerals and vitamins and can be used regularly as a health tonic. However, in cases of inflammation of the kidneys it should not be used unless combined with marshmallow root.

PLANTAIN

Plantago major
Part used: leaves.
Properties: diuretic, blood-purifying, astringent, demulcent.
Energy: cooling. Reduces excess Fire and Water, relieves congested Air.

Plantain is one of the most common European weeds, often aggressively driven out of lawns. The Native Americans noticed that wherever Europeans had lived this new plant appeared and they named it white-man's foot. They were also quick to appreciate its properties and used it to counter the poisons of snake bites. Allow some to remain in a corner of your garden so you have instant access for relief of insect stings, skin infections, wounds, abrasions and burns. For a first-aid poultice, simply chew the leaf for a moment and apply to the skin; for longer-term treatment, wash the area daily with plantain tea.

Used internally in tea form, plantain clears toxins from the blood that give rise to urinary infections, hepatitis and feverish conditions as well as chronic skin complaints such as eczema. Another common weed, cleavers, is similarly diuretic.

RASPBERRY

Rubus idaeus

Part used: leaves.

Properties: astringent, tonic (uterus and stomach), blood regulating (haemostatic and menstrual regulator), mild blood purifier.

Energy: cooling, cleansing. Reduces excess Fire and Water, calms Air but can aggravate if used excessively.

The native European wild raspberry has been used to strengthen the uterus for pregnancy and childbirth. Its stomachic properties also help allay nausea and clean the stomach and intestines. It is high in vitamin C, manganese, iron and other nutrients and can be used regularly as a general tonic. Its mild but effective astringent and blood-purifying actions also clear excess mucous and heat toxins, so use it for colds, flu, sore throats as well as diarrhoea and dysentery, especially in children. Raspberry is often the most easily available and effective treatment for menstrual cramp, heavy or irregular periods and vaginal discharge. Combine with a little ginger to enhance both flavour and action.

RED CLOVER

Trifolium pratense

Part used: flowers.

Properties: blood-purifying, tonic, nutritive, expectorant, antibiotic.

Energy: cooling, tonifying. Clears excess Fire, reduces excess Water.

A small, humble and beautiful wild flower, red clover is one of the most useful and effective herbal medicines. It is a major ingredient in a famous cancer formula, as it cleanses the blood (and thus tissues generally) and is deeply nourishing to the body with its abundance of minerals. It can be taken as a tea for respiratory complaints and mild fevers, especially when the person is young, elderly or debilitated. Use the tea externally for any troublesome skin problem that refuses to heal. For antibiotic action, combine it with others such as echinacea.

ROSEMARY

Rosmarinus officinalis
Part used: leaves.
Properties: aromatic-antiseptic, carminative, nervine-analgesic, circulatory stimulant, diaphoretic, blood regulator (emmenagogue).
Energy: warming, dispersing. Clears excess Fire, reduces excess Water, relieves irritated Air.
Caution: avoid prolonged concentrated use during first trimester of pregnancy. Safe for occasional tea, culinary and short-term uses.

Reach for rosemary as a convenient treatment for many common complaints. Use it for stomach aches, headaches, symptoms of flu, cold or fever and congestion such as constipation or pre-menstrual build-up. Use rosemary generously in cooking to keep the system clean.

SAGE

Salvia officinalis
Part used: leaves.
Properties: astringent, aromatic-antiseptic, stimulant, diuretic, carminative, expectorant.
Energy: warming, dispersing, drying. Clears excess Water and Fire, but may aggravate excess Air (nervousness, dryness).
Caution: avoid prolonged concentrated use during first trimester of pregnancy. Safe for occasional tea, culinary and short-term uses.

Caution: nursing mothers should not take sage.

Sage has very strong astringent and drying properties that indicate its use to clear excess mucous from the nose and lungs, drain sores and ulcers and

LEFT SAGE HAS PUNGENT, AROMATIC LEAVES.

control bleeding. It is most specifically effective for swollen, sore throats when used as a tea and gargle. Another indication is to allay hot flushes during the menopause; for this it can be mixed with rosemary, skullcap and raspberry leaves or motherwort.

The same actions mean the sage should be avoided by nursing mothers, unless of course it is necessary to stop breast-feeding. For this purpose, drink the tea and apply as a fomentation.

SASSAFRAS

Sassafras albidum
Part used: bark of the root.
Properties: blood purifying, diaphoretic, diuretic, tonic (liver), astringent, stimulant.
Energy: warming.
Caution: avoid in strong, acute inflammatory conditions and for long-term use.

BELOW SASSAFRAS IS A USEFUL CLEANSER.

The sassafras tree grows abundantly throughout the south-eastern United States and is much utilized by both Native American peoples and country folk. The bark is deliciously aromatic and flavours the famous root beer beloved by Southerners. A spring tonic tea was traditionally brewed to cleanse the blood and system generally.

Sassafras is most commonly used to treat arthritis, rheumatism and skin complaints, as well as colds and flu, since its blood-purifying and damp-removing actions benefit these conditions.

SKULLCAP

Scutellaria lateriflora
Parts used: flowering stem, leaves.
Properties: nervine. Antispasmodic, relaxing, sedative; anti-inflammatory.
Energy: cooling. Reduces excess Fire; calms and regulates Air.

Skullcap is a reliable, safe nervine for promoting sound sleep and relaxing and restoring the body during stress. It is helpful during drug detoxification to counter the discomforts and anxieties of withdrawal. High in minerals that nourish the nervous tissue, skullcap can be used safely for hypertension, convulsions, epilepsy and neuralgia. It is usually combined with other nervines such as hops, wood betony and passion flower, with perhaps a little ginger to balance and enhance the energy.

ABOVE SKULLCAP HAS ATTRACTIVE PURPLISH-BLUE FLOWERS THAT APPEAR IN SUMMER.

SLIPPERY ELM

Ulmus rubra

Part used: inner bark.

Properties: demulcent, nutritive, anti-inflammatory, expectorant, astringent, vulnerary, tonic, carminative.

Energy: cooling, moistening. Lowers high Fire, clears excess Water (mucous) while strengthening vital fluid base, stabilizes Air.

Slippery elm is one of the most useful herbs and should always be kept on hand. It benefits conditions ranging from superficial wounds and ulcerations to medium-level respiratory congestion, constipation, diarrhoea and colitis, to chronic wasting diseases where there is dryness and weakness.

Slippery elm has an abundance of mucilage that, when mixed with water, thickens and holds the moisture. Whenever tissues are inflamed and irritated, such as in sore throat, stomach acidity or ulcers, bronchitis and asthma, irritable bowel, colitis or gastro-enteritis, picture this herb spreading its thick, soothing and softening coat over them.

LEFT DRIED SLIPPERY ELM BARK IS USED TO TREAT INFLAMMATIONS OF ANY KIND.

For a sore throat, take it as a tea and gargle. For stomach and gastro-intestinal problems, also take as a tea, with a little cinnamon or cloves for flavour and enhanced effect. Use a little in poultices, even if it is not specifically indicated, as it makes a perfect base to hold other herbs. Carry some when travelling for use on minor wounds, stings and abrasions or tummy bugs, and for both diarrhoea and constipation. The tawny-coloured, somewhat fibrous powder is made into a gruel to sustain and strengthen those debilitated with age or chronic, exhausting illnesses and even infants that are not thriving. It builds health and the vital base fluids that sustain the body.

ST JOHN'S WORT

Hypericum perforatum
Parts used: leaves, flowers.
Properties: blood-purifying, anti-inflammatory, nervine, sedative, anti-depressant, tonic and pain relieving, wound healing.
Energy: cooling, calming. Decreases excess Fire and Air.
Caution: Consult your attending medical or herbal practitioner if taking serotonin reuptake inhibitors, non-sedating antihistamines, oral contraceptives, anti-retrovirals, anti-epiletpics, calcium channel blockers, cyclosporine, antibiotics or antifungal medications.

This once common European wildflower has a long history of use in herbal medicine. It was traditionally used to treat wounds, inflammations and ulcers, both internal and external, and painful sciatica, neuralgia and rheumatism. For this latter purpose, a red massage oil is produced by macerating the flowers in vegetable oil for six weeks. This can also be taken internally, a tablespoonful at a time.

More recently, St John's wort has been found to be an effective anti-depressant, lifting and lightening the mood; it is also effective for anxiety, including night terrors in children. It can be used to treat anxiety and depression in menopause. Another contemporary application that is showing results is in the treatment of AIDS; it is prescribed for its nervine and anti-viral (blood-purifying) effects.

THYME

Thymus vulgaris

Parts used: leaves, flowers.

Properties: diaphoretic, nervine, stimulant, carminative, respiratory and lymph cleanser, antiseptic.

Energy: warming, calming. Reduces excess Water, calms Air, clears Fire.

Caution: Avoid prolonged concentrated use during first trimester of pregnancy. Safe for occasional tea, culinary and short-term uses.

BELOW THYME IS USED TO TREAT RESPIRATORY COMPLAINTS.

There are many varieties of thyme but common thyme (*Thymus vulgaris*) is best medicinally. Thyme is excellent when put to work at the first signs of colds or flu, and for any respiratory complaints, coughs and sore throats. It stimulates metabolism and strengthens nerves.

TURMERIC

Curcuma longa

Part used: rhizome.

Properties: blood-purifying and liver tonic, antibacterial, astringent, carminative, vulnerary.

Energy: warming. Reduces excess Fire while strengthening digestion; clears excess Water.

This very common Indian aromatic is in fact a medicine with remarkable powers. Turmeric kills bacteria, counteracts toxins in the blood, cleanses and improves liver function. Apply turmeric paste or a poultice externally to wounds, stings and skin infections or boils, mixed with a little slippery elm. Take it internally as part of a blood-purifying blend, with red clover and/or echinacea for skin problems such as acne.

As well as being a vital ingredient in traditional cooking in India, turmeric is also used to treat even severe blood toxicity and stagnation such as gangrene. Current research shows it has anti-tumour properties and benefits sufferers of rheumatoid arthritis. Turmeric can be used regularly in cooking as a purifying carminative that will aid complete digestion and assimilation, and maintain good health as well as making dishes visually attractive.

VALERIAN
Valeriana officinalis
Part used: root.
Properties: nervine, sedative, relaxant, antispasmodic, analgesic, tonic, diuretic.
Energy: cooling. Calms and stabilizes disturbed Air, while nourishing nerve tissue. Mildly reduces excess Water.
Caution: Do not take simultaneously with alcohol or barbituates.

Valerian is a native European herb that has been used for centuries. The strong aroma – isovaleric acid is the main active constituent – in the roots develops on drying so it is best used when dried. Valerian roots are high in calcium, which nourishes the nerve tissue.

Many people do not like the fragrance of valerian, but it is attractive to cats and other mammals, and cats will instinctively eat the plant when injured; it helps recovery from shock, and is antibacterial and healing.

Valerian is a major herb for the nervous system. It helps the body cope and recover from stress. It relaxes and induces sound sleep. Traditional uses include treatment for hysteria, vertigo, fainting and irritability. Its antispasmodic action helps with muscle and menstrual cramps. Valerian benefits athletes and anyone engaged in aerobics and weight training, as part of preventive and recovery treatment. The powder may be combined with a little ginger, lemon balm or hops and taken as a tea to treat insomnia, cramps and stress.

WHITE PINE BARK
Pinus albicaulis (strobus)
Parts used: inner bark, young needles.
Properties: aromatic, antibacterial, stimulating, expectorant, blood-purifying, diaphoretic.
Energy: warming, stimulating. Clears excess Fire, reduces excess Water.

The white pine of North America is one of the most beautiful trees. It was much used by Native Americans for both food and medicine, the new pine tops having been eaten as a spring tonic, the resin tea used for sore throats and as an expectorant. White pine bark is a major ingredient in the famous Composition Powder developed by Thomsonian herbalism to energize the body and overcome fevers, infections and stagnation. Use the young needles or inner bark in decoction form for respiratory complaints, colds and fevers.

Other pines have similar properties and at one time retreats to sanatoriums in the pine mountains of Germany and Austria were justly popular; walking and breathing the pine-scented air was curative for asthma and other respiratory complaints.

WHITE OAK
Quercus alba
Part used: inner bark.
Properties: astringent, blood-regulating, haemostatic, antibacterial, vulnerary.
Energy: drying, cooling.

The bark of the white and other oaks is high in calcium and tannins, which make it useful for any condition of flaccidity and flux, such as diarrhoea, worms, leucorrhoea and bleeding. It tightens and strengthens any tissue, especially bone, and promotes healing of wounds. Acorns gathered, roasted and ground make an excellent coffee substitute. Walnut leaves have similar properties.

WHITE WILLOW
Salix alba
Part used: inner bark.
Properties: nervine – analgesic pain reliever; blood purifying – anti-inflammatory, antibacterial; astringent.
Energy: cooling. Clears excess Fire, soothes and stabilizes Air, reduces Water.

BELOW THE WILLOW TREE HAS ELEGANT LONG-LEAVED BRANCHES.

White willow bark has traditionally been used by Native Americans and white settlers to treat acute pain and inflammation. It treats the symptoms while clearing the underlying causes of congestion and stagnation. Take it powdered in capsules, tablets or brewed as tea. European willows have similar properties.

WILD YAM
Dioscorea villosa and D. batata
Part used: root.
Properties: tonic – liver and reproductive tissue; nervine antispasmodic; diaphoretic, diuretic, expectorant.
Energy: warming. Reduces excess Fire and Water; calms irritated Air; strengthens vital fluids.

The Central American wild yam provides the source material from which the contraceptive pill, cortisones and sex hormones are derived. Yams are high in plant hormones that support the body's hormone health. Thus, wild yam root is an important constituent of hormone-regulating, herbal formulas. It is also diuretic, liver-cleansing and antispasmodic. It can be used to relieve skin problems, as well as muscular and menstrual cramps. It is a nutritive tonic food treatment for weakness and wasting. Yam is also good for digestive problems as it relieves wind and stagnation of the liver and gall bladder. As an antispasmodic, it can also be used for neuralgic pain.

YARROW

Achillea millefolium
Parts used: leaves and flowers.
Properties: aromatic, bactericidal, diaphoretic, anti-inflammatory, astringent; blood regulating (haemostatic, tonic and emmenagogue).
Energy: warming, drying. Clears excess Fire and Water from blood and digestive tract.

Yarrow has been in use since well before the Christian era. Its Latin name is from Achilles, the hero who could only be wounded in the heel, and the ancient Greeks used yarrow as a wound-healing herb. Like plantain, it was taken to the Americas by settlers, where the Native Americans soon appreciated its uses and found new ones as a blood tonic and regulator given to women after childbirth.

Yarrow clears excess damp mucous from the digestive tract and its diaphoretic and inflammatory action makes it ideal for expelling colds and flu before they take hold. Like all herbs rich in aromatic essential oils, it kills infections and may be used as a tea or poultice on wounds and bleeding. Women may take it as a blood-regulating tonic to ease cramps and excessive bleeding.

SPECIAL ORIENTAL HERBS

The following herbs have been in use in Chinese or Indian medicine for thousands of years and have recently become more well known in the West. Their value is confirmed by scientific research.

ASHWAGHANDA

Withania somnifera
Part used: root.
Properties: rejuvenative and energy tonic; nervine – sedative and tonic; astringent, vulnerary.
Energy: warming, nutritive. Calms and strengthens Air. Increases Fire. Reduces excess Water.

Ashwaghanda, which means 'that which gives the vitality of the horse', is an important tonic herb in Ayurvedic medicine and is now becoming available in the West. Ashwaghanda is similar to ginseng in that it strengthens both tissues and vital energy, especially those of the nervous system, so it is good for the treatment of wasting and deficiency (even in children); the negative effects of overwork and ageing; and for strengthening the immune system through its influence on vital and reproductive fluids. It can be taken with warm milk to promote sound sleep. It could be used as a regular health-maintaining tonic as well as added to formulas for specific weaknesses.

DONG QUAI (OR DANG GUI)
Angelica sinensis
Part used: root.
Properties: blood-regulating, emmenagogue and tonic, antispasmodic, diaphoretic.
Energy: warming, tonifying. Clears excess Fire and stagnant Water, calms and regulates Air. Tonifies blood and the circulatory system.
Caution: avoid in pregnancy and with diarrhoea.

The Chinese angelica is related to our European angelica and has comparable antispasmodic properties but with important additions. As well as relaxing cramps and tension, its warming properties also clear congestion and improve circulation and its nutritive tonifying properties actually improve the quality of the blood. This makes it invaluable for women as it both eases symptoms of the monthly cycle and rebuilds the blood in its aftermath. However, it is not only for women. Dong quai benefits anyone who needs to strengthen the quality and circulation of blood – those with anaemia or symptoms of tiredness – or suffer from cramping pains and tension. It is good added to wound blends as it eases pain while improving circulation of blood to speedily resolve bruising and swelling: this makes it a good recovery medicine for any injury or surgery.

GINSENG
Pariax ginseng
Part used: root.
Properties: tonic to vital energy and immune system, adaptogen, circulatory stimulant.
Energy: warming, nutritive tonic. Revitalizes collapsed energy, combats stress. Strengthens Fire, Air and vital fluids.
Caution: Avoid in conditions of extreme nervous anxiety, hypertension, cardiovascular disease. Those who are in robust health should restrict use to short terms. Other tonics such as Eteudiro coccus, codonopsis and tienchi (*Panax pseudoginseng*) are more appropriate for longer-term tonification.

For 2,000 years or so, the Chinese have appreciated the unique properties of ginseng to enable the body to deal with stress and many other ailments. More than any other herb, it demonstrates the concept of a vital energy tonic. Scientific research has confirmed its remarkable properties. It treats fatigue, convalescence, debility, injury and shock, stress and weakened immunity, and chronic diseases.

We in the West would do well to make ginseng a regular part of our health maintenance programme, as the Chinese do. Small amounts are added to remedies for specific organ weaknesses to enhance the effects of the overall formula and strengthen the organs, especially the lungs and heart. It finds a place in the treatment of AIDS and HIV.

American ginseng (*Panax quinquifolius*) also has tonic properties, which are much appreciated by Chinese medicine.

GOTU KOLA
Centella asiatica
Parts used: leaves and stem.
Properties: rejuvenative tonic, nervine, blood-purifying, diuretic.
Energies: Clears excess Fire, reduces excess Water, strengthens and calms Air. Tonifies immunity and energy.

Gotu kola has similar properties to ashwaghanda, though it works more on the nerve, blood and marrow tissues than hormonal and reproductive fluids. It cleanses the blood, so is good for fevers and skin complaints, and calms and strengthens the nerves.

Ayurveda has a unique classification for herbs called *satvic*. These herbs clear and calm the mind and spirit and promote the qualities needed for spiritual practice. Such herbs, including ashwaghanda, sandalwood and gotu kola, act on the mental and spiritual level as well as the physical. The Indian name for gotu kola is *Brahmi*, or that which leads to knowledge of Brahman, or supreme reality. Such herbs are taken to promote tranquillity and prepare for meditation. For meditation, take gotu kola infusion with honey.

A Note on Safety and Herb-drug Interaction

Evidence shows that herbs are generally safe and have less side-effects than conventional drugs. However, there may be, rarely, an idiosyncratic reaction to a herb.

As more people are using herbs while also taking conventional drug therapy from their medical practitioner, the possibility, largely theoretically, exists that there are certain circumstances in which a herb's properties or the way in which the body processes a herb can affect the way it processes the drug and/or the drug's effect. This is also true of certain foods, for example, grapefruit and coffee. Interactions are uncommon compared with those arising from multi-drug ingestion and usually less serious. To date, herbs known to have this effect include: St. John's wort, ephedra, valerian, kava, licorice, ginkgo, oak bark, sarsaparilla and chasteberry.

This does not mean you cannot take herbs and drug medications together, but if you do, inform both your herbalist and your doctor so that the appropriate monitoring and adjustments can be made. This is especially important if you will be undergoing an operation.

REMEDIES FOR COMMON AILMENTS

CHAPTER SEVEN

The following remedies are suggestions to get you started using herbs. Try them but feel free to adapt them according to your experience, using the Tables on pp.34–35 and the Materia Medica. See Chapter 5 on how to prepare the herbs. Creating your own blends and discovering what works for you, your family and friends is enjoyable and satisfying. For best results, herbs should be used with a cleansing, health-improving diet.

Herbs for Digestive Ailments

ACID STOMACH, INDIGESTION, HEARTBURN
Take one warm cup of any of the following half an hour before eating:
- Tea decoction of a sweet, warming blend: equal parts fennel, licorice, fenugreek, anise, ¼ part slippery elm or dandelion root.
- Light, minty tea: equal parts meadowsweet, peppermint or spearmint or catnip, ½ part rosemary.
- Slice of lemon squeezed in 8fl oz (227ml) hot water.

COLIC OR CRAMPING PAINS IN THE INTESTINAL TRACT
Take the following half an hour before eating or when needed:
- Tea decoction of equal parts ginger, chamomile, catnip.

- For children and babies: equal parts catnip, spearmint or peppermint and fennel. Alternatively, combine dill with chamomile or lemon balm.

CONSTIPATION
- A typical blend would be raspberry leaves, licorice, slippery elm and fennel. Add ginger, black pepper or cayenne for Water types.
- Taking 3tbsp of olive oil and 6tbsp of lemon juice in grapefruit or orange juice first thing in the morning is helpful.

DIARRHOEA
- Fruits high in pectin such as apples and bananas are useful, when grated, mashed and combined with warming, astringent herbs such as cinnamon, allspice and nutmeg.
- Tea of equal parts mullein or raspberry, slippery elm, chamomile or catnip, and meadowsweet with ¼ part ginger or black pepper. Honey is also beneficial.

HYPOGLYCAEMIA
A condition in which an over-secretion of insulin into the blood burns off available blood sugar, causing temporary fatigue, coldness, headaches, irritability, palpitations or dizziness. Stress and hereditary factors may play a part.
- Ensure adequate complex carbohydrate and protein intake through good diet. Brown rice and mung or aduki beans are very beneficial.
- Blend equal parts dandelion root, burdock root, licorice root and skullcap. Take these in tea or powdered form, three times daily.

IRRITABLE BOWEL AND COLITIS
- A combination of bowel-cleansing and tonic herbs with equal the amount of demulcents benefits this condition tremendously.
- Tea or powders in capsules or pills of equal parts licorice root, raspberry, fennel, barberry and rhubarb

ABOVE RASPBERRY.

root. Mix these, then add an equivalent amount of slippery elm or marshmallow root.

Caution: avoid barberry and rhubarb root during pregnancy.

- Take a nervine tea such as chamomile or lemon balm and wood betony, catnip and vervain.

If symptoms persist or if there is any bleeding, consult a trained herbalist or medical doctor.

NAUSEA OR VOMITING

- Ginger tea.
- Peppermint tea.
- Juice of a lemon slice in warm water.
- Make a tea of equal parts cinnamon, cardamom, peppermint or clove or nutmeg.
- Michael Tierra recommends the following combination: three parts cinnamon, one part each of clove, cardamom and nutmeg. Mix and use ¼–½tsp per cup of water for the brew, or mix powders with honey and eat one teaspoon as needed.

Herbs for Respiratory Ailments

ASTHMA

- Chronic cases should be referred to a professional herbalist. In mild cases or only occasional and mild crisis, refer to the remedies for colds and flu and coughs, p.103.
- During an attack, take a hot tea of ½tsp each of ginger and licorice powder. Rub warm sesame oil into the chest.
- Between attacks, cleanse the system with a tea of equal parts of thyme, nettle and skullcap. Drink a cup 30 minutes after meals.
- Make a herb pillow with nervine and aromatic herbs, for example lavender and basil.

ABOVE GINGER.

EARACHE
- Make a herbal oil from garlic, ginger or mullein. Dip a piece of cotton wool in the oil and plug the ear. Renew as needed.
- A poultice made with slippery elm or marshmallow root powder spread around the outside of the ear has proved very effective.
- Take echinacea capsules every one to two hours.

COLDS AND FLU
- Adopt a cleansing diet for one to three days. Rest.
- Take a tablespoon of garlic oil or garlic capsules every hour. Alternatively, take two echinacea, thyme or golden seal (singly or combined) capsules every two hours during the day.
- Take trikatu blend, a combination derived from Ayurvedic tradition. It is also useful for sinus congestion, hay fever and other respiratory allergies. To make trikatu (adapted by Michael Tierra, *see* p.122), mix two parts anise, one part ginger and one part black pepper powder, blended with honey to form a paste. Take 1tsp before meals.
- Tea of equal parts of the following: elderflower and peppermint; thyme and basil; white pine and ginger; yarrow, raspberry and black pepper. Add honey to taste.

COUGHS
- To the herbs mentioned for colds, add expectorants and demulcens: e.g. coltsfoot, comfrey leaves, elecampane, mullein, hyssop, thyme.
- A cough syrup made of a concentrated tea of thyme mixed with raw sugar and honey has been found effective in stubborn cases and in whooping cough: infuse 1pt (570ml) of strong thyme tea and strain. Add 1¾lb (0.79kg) of raw sugar, heat gently in a covered pot, stirring at intervals, until the sugar is dissolved. Skim off the surface accumulation. Cool and store. Take 1tbs as needed.

External Treatments for a Cough
- Steam inhalation as described on p.54 is also a valuable treatment for colds and coughs.

- Mustard packs (a poultice of mustard powder and flour or slippery elm) on the chest. Rub chest with olive oil first and remove the pack as the skin begins to redden. Repeat at intervals as needed. Use a mustard or cayenne foot bath.
- Chest and upper back massages with blends of two drops each of two essential oils in 3tsp or 15ml vegetable oil. Choose from eucalyptus, chamomile, thyme, lavender, pine or cypress.

RESPIRATORY ALLERGIES, HAY FEVER
- Treat as for colds. Use trikatu blend (*see* p.103). Drink hot lemon and honey. Take a powdered blend of ephedra, thyme or pine tops combined with marshmallow root, juniper, burdock root, parsley, cayenne or black pepper and golden seal.
- Another helpful combination, from David Frawley and Dr Lad (*see* p.122), is turmeric powder warmed in butter with raw sugar; cool, and take one teaspoon of the paste every ½–1 hour during attacks.
- For red, itchy eyes, bathe eyes in a wash of chamomile, eyebright, raspberry or chrysanthemum-flower tea. Soak a cotton wool pad in the tea and place over the eyes; even a cool black teabag can be used to great effect.

SINUS CONGESTION
- Garlic in capsule form or raw taken regularly clears this condition for many people. Eat a paste with pressed raw garlic mixed with honey.
- A very strong combination is a blend of equal parts grated horseradish, chopped onion and garlic and a pinch of cayenne. Macerate in apple-cider vinegar for three days. Strain and take 1tbs one to three times a day.
- Trikatu blend (*see* p.103) is effective. Take just before meals.
- Anti-infectious and lymph-clearing herbs are needed, along with soothing demulcents to allay pain. Follow a cleansing diet for one to three days. Rest.
- Gargle with a warm tea of sage or red sage and raspberry leaves

with honey. Drink the tea every ½–1 hour. If possible, take echinacea capsules or tea every hour.
- A good sore throat remedy is to blend: 4tbs honey, 6tbs lemon juice, 4tbs apple-cider vinegar, ⅓ clove garlic pressed or ¼tsp powder, ¼tsp ginger. Process to blend and take as a gargle or syrup. For a drink, add hot water up to 8fl oz (227ml).

HERBS FOR URINARY AILMENTS

Adopt a cleansing diet for a few days, and drink lots of pure water.

CYSTITIS
- Drink a tea made from diuretic and urinary cleansing herbs: equal parts dandelion root, nettles, parsley, chickweed, couchgrass, yarrow, cleavers.
- Along with the tea, take anti-infectants such as golden seal and echinacea in capsules. Add to the tea demulcents such as marshmallow root, slippery elm. Drink eight or more glasses of pure cranberry, coconut or pomegranate juice daily; and/or eat live, natural yoghurt. Rest.
- If the condition is recurrent and the person feels tired and has a low-grade fever, elimination and tonification treatment should be taken once the acute attack has cleared.

WATER RETENTION
The remedies suggested aim to improve kidney excretion, to clear any fluid congestion, to promote assimilation of food and elimination of waste and to clean the blood and lymph and promote circulation. Water types are most easily prone to this pattern, though it is found in all types. Do not confuse it with the deeper oedema based on heart and kidney weakness, for which professional treatment is needed.
- Take a digestion-promoting combination given under that section. Trikatu blend with meals is excellent.

- Drink a mild diuretic tea that will not over-stimulate the kidneys.
- Diuretic tea combinations: equal parts lemongrass, fennel or coriander or parsley; chickweed, couch grass, cleavers, juniper berries. Water types include a pinch of ginger. Air types should take the tea hot; Fire types take it room temperature; Water types warm with honey.
- Lymph and blood-cleansing herbs can be included in a blend – for example, red clover, chaparral, burdock, echinacea – along with circulatory stimulants such as ginger, cayenne and black pepper.

Herbs for Skin Ailments

Skin ailments usually indicate imbalances deeper in the system. Topical remedies must be combined with systemic treatment according to constitutional type.

ACNE

Contributing factors are poor diet (junk food such as chocolate, fried foods, coffee, tea, refined flour and sugar products), stress, liver congestion and hormonal imbalance.

- Have daily steam facials with cleansing herbs such as sage, eucalyptus, rosemary and thyme.
- Apply soothing ointments of calendula or comfrey; antiseptic and cleansing aloe vera gel; a paste made from turmeric and slippery elm mixed with a little water.
- Internally, take a tea of one to three of these blood-purifying and kidney- and liver-cleansing herbs: alfalfa, echinacea, red clover, burdock, dandelion, licorice, nettle, sassafras, yarrow, yellow dock, plantain and cleavers. Drink one cup three times a day.
- Avoid foods that stimulate the Fire humour: fried foods, greasy and rich foods, tomatoes and hot spices.
- Take a hormone blend such as the one suggested under Reproductive Ailments (*see* pp.114–118).

ATHLETE'S FOOT
- Go barefoot if possible; wear cotton socks. Take daily foot baths in tea of rosemary and thyme with 2tbsp lemon juice or cider vinegar.
- Massage feet with essential oils of lemon, tea tree, eucalyptus, lavender, thyme or rosemary – up to four drops diluted in about 3tsp or 15ml of carrier vegetable oil.
- Internally, take garlic or echinacea capsules.

ALLERGIES, SKIN RASHES, INSECT BITES, STINGS
- Apply a slippery elm or marshmallow root poultice or fomentation and drink a tea of chamomile, calendula or plantain. Also bathe the area with these herb teas and take a herb tea bath.
- Apply aloe vera gel; marigold, comfrey or chickweed ointment.

DANDRUFF
- Correct the diet, cutting out junk and processed foods. Try a vitamin and mineral supplement or take kelp tablets. Check that your shampoo is mild and natural.
- After shampooing, rinse with a tea made with rosemary, nettles, nasturtium combined with half the amount of apple-cider vinegar. When possible, massage scalp with warm olive oil combined with two drops of rosemary essential oil.
- Daily, drink nettle and sage or rosemary tea to cleanse the blood and improve circulation.

ABOVE ROSEMARY.

ECZEMA
Treatment for eczema needs to be discussed with a professional herbalist, but for temporary relief or mild conditions, try the following.
- Apply oil of evening primrose.
- Bathe the area with tea of marigold, comfrey leaves, chamomile, marshmallow root.
- Macerate in oil: lavender, chamomile, calendula, comfrey or marshmallow leaves and apply twice daily.

- An ointment made with balm of Gilead buds is very effective.
- Internally, take teas of blood-purifying, heat-releasing herbs such as burdock root, red clover, yarrow, marshmallow root, calendula, elderflower, nettle or chamomile; and nervine teas to allay anxiety and stress: chamomile, skullcap, lemon balm, catnip, vervain or wood betony.

EYE INFLAMMATIONS AND STYES
- Make a tea with slippery elm or marshmallow root and eyebright, calendula, borage, elderflower, honeysuckle flower, fennel powder or chamomile. Strain and cool. Soak a cotton wool ball in the tea and apply to the eyelid and area around the eye; give an eyewash using an eyecup.
- Take echinacea capsules for a few days to boost the immune system.

WOUNDS, INFECTIONS, BOILS, ABRASIONS
- Apply aloe vera gel or a poultice or ointment of plantain, comfrey, marigold, St John's wort, yarrow, slippery elm, lemon balm, chamomile, thyme or self-heal.
- When in the wild, make an emergency poultice by chewing the leaves of one of these or other recognized wound herbs, and place them on the wound.
- Honey is another antiseptic first-aid remedy.

BURNS
- Aloe vera gel is excellent.
- Apply comfrey or marigold ointment.
- For an excellent combination for severe burns from Dr Christopher (*see* p.17): in a blender, mix equal parts wheatgerm oil and honey. Gradually add chopped fresh or dry (powdered) comfrey leaves to form a paste. Apply cool and leave on the burn WITHOUT disturbing it until the skin underneath has healed. Remoisten at intervals with comfrey and chickweed tea. This also relieves itching. Avoid exposure of new skin to sunlight for one year.

HERBS FOR INSECT REPELLENTS

- Massage into the skin a vegetable oil blended with three of the following essential oils, two drops each in 1tbs carrier oil: lavender, thyme, basil, lemon, geranium, bay, citronella.

HERBS FOR CIRCULATORY AND LYMPHATIC AILMENTS

CHILBLAINS
- Take tepid foot baths with 2tbs ginger, mustard or cayenne powder. Apply crushed onion.
- Rub the area with comfrey, or calendula ointment. Avoid the temptation to apply heat immediately as this will only worsen the situation with sudden dilation. Gentle re-warming is called for.
- To strengthen the circulation and capillaries, drink a daily tea of ginger, marjoram, cloves, cumin, thyme, hawthorn berries, nettle or buckwheat. Take garlic capsules daily.

SWOLLEN GLANDS
- Tea or powders in capsules or pills of lymph-clearing herbs: equal parts of mullein, echinacea, garlic, dandelion root and red clover.
- Poke root is a specific, but must not be used during pregnancy.
- Apply a poultice of astringents such as oak bark, walnut leaves or mullein with fennel, fenugreek, marshmallow root or slippery elm powders over the area.

SWOLLEN ANKLES OR KNEES
- Lightly apply essential oil blends of cypress, cedarwood or fennel, diluted in vegetable oil.
- Apply a salt pack: warm the salt in the oven, enough to cover the area to ¼in (6mm); wrap it in a tea-towel and apply over the area. Leave for an hour or overnight.

- Take a diuretic tea blend to reduce excess damp such as ginger with dandelion, burdock, cleavers and horsetail.

GENERAL COLDNESS
- Include ginger or black pepper, and cardamom in your daily drinks and foods. Massage sesame oil into the body two or three times a week and on the soles of the feet at bedtime.

Herbs for Muscles and Joints

ARTHRITIS
This is often a condition of excess damp and toxicity accumulating in the fluid and tissues around the joints producing stiffness, low-grade inflammation and consequent soreness. There may be an acute phase with greater inflammation, swelling, heat and redness.
- Local applications: warm stiff, sore joints with fresh ginger juice: grate some root and squeeze the juice into some vegetable oil, rub into the area. Use two handfuls of Epsom salts in the bath.
- Internally, take blood-purifying and circulation herbs to warm and disperse. For example, equal parts alfalfa, red clover, mullein, skullcap, chickweed or nettles, parsley and hibiscus. Take one cup two to three times a day. The tea may need to be taken for about three months, alternating the herbs in the blend every week.
- When there is acute pain, inflammation, redness and swelling, apply a cooling poultice of marshmallow root.

BACK PAIN
While back pain may be structural in origin, it can also be due to a weakening or stress of kidney function.
- Use the remedies for sciatica and also take a kidney-tonifying blend such as the following. Tea or decoction: one part each of marshmallow root, parsley root or leaf, cleavers, horsetail and juniper berries with ¼ part ginger.

ABOVE CLEAVERS.

STRAIN OR SPRAIN

Follow this **RICE** procedure when the injury occurs:

1. **R**est
2. Apply cold in the form of **I**ce or frozen peas
3. Apply a **C**ompression bandage
4. **E**levate the injury so blood flows toward the heart.

- Additionally, apply a fomentation, oil or poultice of yarrow, comfrey or St John's wort tea mixed with blood-moving herbs such as ginger or dong quai. A comfrey poultice will also help. Drink a tea of comfrey leaf, St John's wort leaves and walnut leaves if available. (Commercially produced homeopathic remedies such as Arnica 6 and Bach Flower Star of Bethlehem or Rescue Remedy may be taken.)
- In contrast to the cold treatment recommended above, Chinese medicine recommends applying heat. Heat is said to promote blood circulation, so clearing swelling, pain and stasis sooner.

SCIATICA

This is pain along the sciatic nerve. The nerve emerges from the sacrum to enervate the legs and feet. Pain is often due to disc prolapse, especially at the fifth lumbar vertebra, or to structural or postural imbalance affecting the vertebrae, involving the muscles of the buttocks, sacrum and pelvis. A remedial massage therapist, chiropractor or osteopath should be consulted; specific exercises may be given to improve the situation. The following herbal remedies have also proved helpful to many people, as poor diet and lack of exercise can cause blood and lymph stagnation that accumulates in the tissues in this area and provokes or contributes to the pain.

- Externally: apply a 2tsp ginger and 1tsp turmeric paste, warm, to the area. St John's wort oil may be rubbed into the area for temporary relief. Use an essential oil massage blend choosing three of the following: lavender, rosemary, chamomile, peppermint, black pepper, eucalyptus or wintergreen.
- Baths with these herbs as teas are also good.

- Internally: drink willow bark, nettle or chamomile tea. Take St John's wort tincture.

HERBS FOR NERVOUS AILMENTS

Refer to nervine action herbs (*see* tables, pp.43–46).

ANXIETY
- Take a tea of skullcap, borage, chamomile and/or lemon balm.
- Basil tea and sandalwood essential oil used as a massage rub or room scent promote a calm but alert mind.

DEPRESSION
- Borage tea conveys courage. Lemon balm is an excellent traditional remedy for melancholia, that feeling of dejection and withdrawal from the world. Lemon balm tea from fresh leaves is best. However, if this is not possible use other mints such as spearmint. Lemon balm is both relaxing to the nerves and uplifting to the spirits, as are most of the aromatic herbs – basil, rosemary, lavender and many others.
- According to Rudolf Weiss (*see* p.122), St John's wort is used by European herbalists to treat depression: take as a tea twice a day. It has a cumulative effect so may be necessary to take for several weeks before a change is noticed. Adding ginger to a blend will help energy to circulate and break up stagnation. Herbs used regularly can be effective.
- Refer to the section on reproductive ailments (*see* p.114–118).

HEADACHES
The head can be a focal point for the expression of imbalances elsewhere, for example stomach upsets, constipation, excess water or lymph congestion and liver congestion. Issues of stress or nervous tension can cause headaches. Such background causes should be

given treatment by referring to the appropriate section. Diet may be a factor so food therapy may be useful.

- Internally, take a tea of one to three of meadowsweet, willow bark, poplar bark, lime flowers, peppermint, chamomile, skullcap, rosemary, ginger, wood betony, valerian, basil, lemon balm, passion flower or sage.
- A tea of cumin and coriander is also helpful for headaches based on liver congestion.
- For occipital headaches (at the back of the head) take a colon-cleansing blend (e.g. flax or senna) at bedtime with warm milk.
- Meadowsweet, willow bark and poplar bark all contain salicylic acid, the active ingredient in aspirin, and will relieve pain.
- Externally, apply a ginger paste (powdered ginger mixed with a little turmeric and water) to the forehead and sinuses for sinus headaches and behind the ears for occipital headaches.

ABOVE VALERIAN.

FATIGUE AND STRESS

- Take a nervine tea of one to three of the following: skullcap, wood betony, chamomile, catnip, lemon balm, rosemary or vervain.
- Tonify the glandular system with the hormone blend given for reproductive ailments, adding ginseng.
- Herbs to build the quality of the blood may also be beneficial: take a daily tea, equal parts of one to three of the following: nettles, yarrow, burdock, yellow dock, alfalfa, dong quai or comfrey leaves.

INSOMNIA

- During the afternoon and early evening, drink a tea of one to three of the following: valerian, catnip, lemon balm, lime flowers, hops, wood betony, passionflower, skullcap or chamomile.
- Make a herbal pillow with the following herbs: hops, lavender, passionflower, skullcap and valerian. Place it in your pillowcase.
- Apply a few drops of lavender or other relaxant essential oil (e.g. marjoram, ylang ylang) on a handkerchief attached to the pillow.

Herbs for Female Reproductive Ailments

Herbs have much help to offer in creating and maintaining balance: some are used for their cleansing and tonifying action on the organs, blood and lymph; others relax and relieve cramp and pain. There are herbs that contain plant hormones that are precursors to human hormones: their molecular structure is very similar and the body can use components of them to regulate its own functions. Cleansing and balancing on the physical level will be reflected in feelings of well-being throughout the body.

EXCESSIVE BLEEDING

Energetically, this is considered a condition of excess heat in the blood. Causes may include an excess of warming herbs and beverages, hot spices, sour foods, salt, alcohol and, at a more subtle level, hot emotions such as anger or resentment. Fire types are perhaps a little more prone to this. However, excessive bleeding can also be due to other factors such as incomplete (and unknown) miscarriage, cervical erosion, endometriosis, polyps and tumours, so professional medical advice should always be consulted.

- For the relief of minor discomfort caused by a heavy period, take blood-cleansing and cooling herbs such as tea of red clover, yarrow and peppermint, together with astringents such as raspberry leaves and shepherd's purse.
- Blood regulators such as dong quai are also important, as are hormone balancers. Adopt a cleansing diet for three weeks.

LEFT SHEPHERD'S PURSE.

IRREGULAR PERIODS
- For irregular periods, take a tea of one to three of the following herbs: yarrow, motherwort, raspberry, lemon balm, lady's mantle, chamomile, thyme and peppermint, plus blood regulators such as dong quai.

HOT FLUSHES
- Take a tea of rosemary, sage and lemon balm or peppermint. Drink one cup three times a day. Take a hormone combination, such as the one suggested on p.116, and a blood-purifying blend.

PERIOD PAIN
If severe and prolonged, this can indicate a more serious condition, so consult a trained practitioner or doctor.
- Use warming, antispasmodic and blood-regulating herbs that relieve cramp, such as cramp bark, turmeric, fennel, angelica, dong quai, wild yam, ginger and chamomile.
- Agnus castus is especially helpful as it increases the level of progesterone, a hormone that prevents uterine contractions. Drink a tea combining it with raspberry and the antispasmodic herbs for a week before the onset of the period.
- Taking a hormone combination, such as the one for premenstrual tension, is also advised. Take two capsules three times a day.

PRE-MENSTRUAL TENSION
Symptoms of bloating, sore breasts, headaches and irritability around the start of the period can be related to lymph or blood stagnation and general congestion.
- Take a herb tea to clear excess water and cleanse the blood and bowels. Support the reproductive organs with a daily tea of raspberry leaves, motherwort and/or squaw vine. Include a warming, circulating herb such as ginger.
- For temporary relief of headache, take a nervine such as rosemary, willow bark or skullcap.

HORMONAL CHANGES

The sexual turning points of life, from puberty to the menopause, can be extremely stressful. Using the following hormone blend periodically through these years can minimize any negative effects and leave the body stronger. Take it for three weeks at a time.

- Hormone blend: a basic combination to use for good hormone function at the life-changes and for menstrual problems is equal parts kelp, dong quai, ginseng, sarsaparilla, agnus castus, wild yam, licorice, false unicorn, fennel and black cohosh. Combine with a 1/4 amount of ginger and a nervine such as chamomile or vervain. Take in capsule, tea or decoction form three times daily for three weeks. Repeat as needed. For period problems, take three times a day for one week before the period every month for at least three months.

PREGNANCY AND CHILDBIRTH

Herbs can be very helpful to counteract the minor discomforts of pregnancy and to strengthen the muscles for childbirth. Pregnancy is not the time to embark on a cleansing programme, though it is a good idea to do so before conception.

- For nausea, take a pinch of ginger in weak tea or hot water with a slice of lemon.
- Drink raspberry leaf tea regularly throughout pregnancy. In the last six weeks, begin to tone the muscles with a tea of raspberry leaves, squaw vine, or motherwort.
- Prepare the vaginal area by massaging wheatgerm oil (1–2tsp) daily into the perineum and vulva.
- During childbirth, essential oils such as jasmine, lavender, chamomile and clary sage may be used in massage and as room scents to comfort the mother.
- To promote lactation, drink fennel, dill or basil tea. For engorged breasts, apply a sage compress. Apply calendula or comfrey ointment to sore nipples.

- To calm a restless baby, the nursing mother can drink chamomile or other nervine teas. The effects will be conveyed to the baby through the milk. An older infant may be given a teaspoon of chamomile tea before sleep.
- Herbs to be avoided during pregnancy include golden seal, poke root, dong quai, angelica, barberry, hyssop, senna, turkey rhubarb, rue and vervain. The following culinary herbs should be used with some caution, especially in the first trimester; they are safe for occasional or short-term use and in cooking, but the worry is that with prolonged or concentrated use their stimulating properties may provoke a miscarriage or premature labour: fennel, fenugreek, cayenne, garlic, thyme, sage, marjoram, juniper, cinnamon, parsley and peppermint. On the other hand, they may be taken at the end of term to help prepare for labour.

MENOPAUSE
- Take the hormone blend and combine with a nervine tea. (*See also* hot flushes, p.115).
- Scanty flow: take a tea or powders in capsules of warming, blood moving, emmenagogue (promoting menstrual discharge) herbs such as dong quai, fennel, vervain and yarrow, along with a reproductive tonic such as raspberry or motherwort.

VAGINAL DISCHARGE
In simple cases this is usually due to an imbalance in the acidity of the area, often brought on by antibiotics, a diet too high in sugar, processed and acid-forming foods, or to thrush (a fungal infection).
- To relieve itching, apply calendula or chickweed ointment, or simply olive or wheatgerm oil. Vulval itching is an important symptom in diabetes, so repeated or prolonged itching suggests a consultation with a doctor would be in order.
- Douche with yoghurt mixed with the same amount of water, or with yellow dock tea.

- Vaginal pessaries with essential oil of tea tree and lavender are now available and may be used.
- Take herbal antibiotics such as echinacea or golden seal in tea or capsule form.

HERBS FOR MALE AILMENTS

PROSTATE SWELLING

This condition appears in some men as they pass into their middle and later years. In the beginning stages and in mild cases, there is pain or burning on urination due to the swelling of the gland and consequent pressure on the urethra.

- Take the following hormone combination in tea or powdered, capsule form: juniper berries, couchgrass, horsetail and hydrangea root. Take echinacea and/or golden seal.

ABOVE JUNIPER BERRIES.

PUBERTY AND/OR STRESS

- Men can also benefit from the recommended hormone combination during puberty, (*see* p.116), in middle and older age and whenever affected by a time of stress. It strengthens glandular function in both sexes and enhances vitality and vigour.

HERBS FOR FEVERS AND INFECTIONS

Fevers and infections, when temporary, are due to a combination of excess Fire (heat-toxins and pathogens) or Water (phlegm and mucous) in the blood or lymph that allow pathogens to thrive in this milieu. The body raises its temperature to burn off the excess and destroy the bacteria or virus.

- Choose blood-purifying, diaphoretic and antibiotic herbs. Herbs to use in teas or capsules include golden seal, echinacea, burdock, yarrow, garlic, thyme and sage.
- For local external skin infections or boils, take the recommended herbs internally and also apply a poultice of plantain, slippery elm, marshmallow root and golden seal or thyme.

If fevers recur often, consult a qualified herbalist or doctor.

Herbs for First Aid

Keep some herbs and preparations on hand for emergencies, while travelling and for the most common complaints.

- Chickweed, comfrey or calendula ointment for wounds and sores.
- Cayenne tincture for shock, bleeding and fainting.
- Herbal liniment: from equal parts juniper, basil and ginger. Use for wounds, muscular aches and sprains.

Herb tea blends can be used for many common ailments.

- For colds and flu: elderflower and peppermint; chamomile and lemon balm.
- For pain relief: willow bark and rosemary; meadowsweet and ginger.
- For 'stomach bug' (short-term gastroenteritis): ginger, slippery elm or licorice and cinnamon.
- For soothing and sleep: catnip, hops, chamomile, wood betony, vervain or lime flowers.
- For cramps: catnip, ginger and fennel.
- For nausea: ginger and peppermint.
- Herbal antibiotics: equal parts echinacea and golden seal powders in capsules.

Useful Addresses

The following list details the addresses of some established training institutions. Contact these for referral to your local herbalist.

UK

Association of Master Herbalists
107 Brampton Road
Cambridge CB1 3HJ
Tel: 01223 212744
pete.j-m@virgin.net

Ayurvedic Medical Association
95 Westwood Lane
Welling, Bexley
Kent DA16 2HJ
Tel: 020 8303 4175

British Society of Chinese Medicine
Clerkenwell Building
Archway Campus 2–0
Highgate Hill
London N19 5LW
Tel: 020 7272 6888/

College of Practising Phytotherapists
London Clinic of Phytotherapy
Gemini House
180–182 Bermondsey Street
London SE1 3TQ
Tel: 020 7378 8888/01968 679080 (& fax)
peter@conwayacott.jambag.co.uk

International Register of Consulting Herbalists and Homeopaths
Ifanca James
IRCH Registered Office
32 King Edwards Road
Swansea SA1 4LL
01792 655886
office@irch.org

National Institute of Medical Herbalists
NIMH Registered Office
56 Longbrook Street
Exeter Devon EX4 6AH
01886 821026

Register of Chinese Herbal Medicine
46 Clarence Road
Birmingham B13 9UH
Tel: 0121 442 2059
nick@lampert.freeserve.co.uk

Tara Rokpa: College of Tibetan Medicine
127 Elmhurst Mansions
Edgeley Road
London SW4 6EX
Tel: 020 7622 0164

USEFUL ADDRESSES

Unified Register of Herbal
Practitioners
94 Grosvenor Road
London SW1V 3LF
020 7834 3579

For residential courses in
Ayurvedic living:
Practical Ayurveda
27 Lankers Drive, North Harrow
Middlesex HA2 7PA
Tel: 020 8866 5944

For information on the current
legal status and news of herbal
medicine in the UK and Europe,
contact the European Herbal
Practitioners Association
website: www.users.globalnet.
co.uk/~ehpa/
The EHPA, newsletter,
Frankincense, is available for a
£4.00 subscription from
Midsummer Cottage
Nether Wescott
Chipping Norton
Oxon OX7 6SD

United States and Australia
To obtain a list of established
and accredited training
institutions please contact the
following professional
organisations, then contact a
registered institution for a list of
qualified graduate practicing in
your local area.

American Herbalists Guild
1931 Gaddis Rd.
Canton GA 30115 USA
ahgoffice@earthlink.com
www.americanherbalist.com

The National Herbalists
Association of Australia
33 Reserve Street
Annandale NSW 2038
Tel: +61 2 9560 7077
Fax: +61 2 9560 7055
email: nhaa@nhaa.org.au
web site: nhaa.org.au

Useful Websites
www.pubmed.com (go to link for
alternative medicine, then herbs)
www.planetherbs.com
www.vedanet.com
www.webmd.com

Further Reading

Bartram, Thomas, *Bartram's Encycopedia of Herbal Medicine*, Robinson, 1998

Christopher, Dr John, *The School of Natural Healing*, Biworld Publishing, Provo, Utah, 1976

Grieve, M, *A Modern Herbal*, Jonathan Cape, 1931. Recent editions by Savva Publishing, Adelaide, 1985

Hoffman, David, *The New Holistic Herbal*, Element Books, Shaftesbury, Dorset, 1983

Lad, Dr Vasant, and Frawley, David, *The Yoga of Herbs*, Lotus Press, Santa Fe, New Mexico, 1986

Levy, Juliette de Bairchi, *The llustrated Herbal Handbook*, Faber and Faber, 1974

Lust, John, *The Herb Book*, Bantam Books, New York, 1974

Lust, John and Tierra, Michael, *The Natural Remedy Bible*, Pocket Books, New York, 1990

Mabey, Richard (Ed), *The Complete New Herbal*, Penguin Books, 1991

Messegué, Maurice, *Of Men and Plants*, Weidenfeld and Nicolson, London, 1972

Nissim, Rina, *Natural Healing in Gynaecology*, Pandora Press, London and New York, 1986

Pedersen, Mark, *Nutritional Herbology*, Pedersen Publishing, Bountiful, Utah, 1987

Stuart, Malcolm, *The Encyclopedia of Herbs and Herbalism*, Caxton/Macdonald & Co, 1989

Teegarden, Ron, *Chinese Tonic Herbs*, Japan Publications Inc., Tokyo and New York, 1984

Tierra, Lesley, *The Herbs of Life*, Crossing Press, Freedom, California, 1992

Tierra, Michael, *The Way of Herbs*, Orenda/Unity Press, 1980
– *Planetary Herbology*, Lotus Press, Santa Fe, New Mexico, 1988

Weiss, Rudolf Fritz, *Herbal Medicine*, Beaconsfield Publishers Ltd, Beaconsfield, UK

Herbalgram, The Journal of the American Botanical Council and the Herb Research Foundation, P.O.Box 144345, Austin, Texas 78714-4345, Tel. 512 926-4900, www.herbalgram.org

Sources of Herbal Supplies

Many health-food shops supply good quality dried herbs, and some also have other more strictly medicinal herbs. Many companies also supply herbs by mail order. You may also find ethnic food shops that carry the traditional herbs of a particular culture.

The Ayurvedic
Trading Company
East–West Centre
10 High Street
Glastonbury
Somerset, BA6 9DU
Tel: 01458 833 382
www.eastwestcentre.com

G. Baldwin & Co
173 Walworth Road
London SE17 1RW
Tel: 020 7703 5550

East-West Herbs
Neal's Yard
London WC2H 9PD
Tel: 020 7379 1312

Galen Herbal
Supplies Ltd
Unit 17, St. David's
Industrial Estate
Pengam, Blackwood
Gwent NP12 1SW

Hambledon Herbs
Court Farm
Milverston
Somerset 7AH 1NF
Tel: 01823 401104

Herbs of Grace
5A Lanwades
Business Park
Kennett, Newmarket,
Suffolk, CB8 7YA
Tel: 01638 750140
Sales@herbsofgrace.co.uk

Malcolm Simmonds
Herbal Supplies
3 Burton Villas
Hove
Sussex BN3 6FN
Tel: 01273 202401

Napiers Herbalists
18 Bistro Place
Edinburgh EH1 1EZ
Tel: 0131 225 5542

Neal's Yard
Remedies
Neal's Yard
Covent Garden,
London WC2H 9PD
Tel: 020 7379 7222

Pukka Herbs
1 The Mews
Church Rd
Leighwoods
Bristol BS 83PG
Tel: 0117 9744811
www.pukkaherbs.com

Specialists Herbal
Supplies, Freepost
Hove
Sussex BN3 6BR
Sales@herbalsupplies.com

Star Child
3 The Courtyard
2–4 High Street
Glastonbury
Tel: 01342 282 2312
Somerset BA6 9DU
Tel: 01458 834663

Vital Force
Hartswood
Marsh Green
Hartfield
E. Sussex TN7 4ET

Glossary

Adaptogen: agent that enables the body to deal with and recover from stress and disease.
Allopathic medicine: 'orthodox' medicine, in which drugs are used to oppose and alleviate disease.
Analgesic: pain-relieving.
Anodyne: pain-relieving.
Antibiotic: combats infection.
Anti-inflammatory: reduces swelling and pain due to irritation, infection or injury.
Antipyretic: reduces fever.
Antiseptic: controls infection and helps prevent tissue degeneration.
Antispasmodic: relieves cramp.
Astringent: contracts, tightens and binds tissues.
Calcination: process of refining by roasting or burning.
Carminative: expels gas trapped in intestines, improves digestion.
Contraindication: any factor that makes it unwise to pursue a certain line of treatment.
Demulcent: soothing agent that protects mucous membranes and relieves irritation.
Detoxicant: eliminates poisons.
Diaphoretic: causes increase in perspiration and release of waste via the skin.
Distillation: process of extracting essence of plants by heating to vapour, condensing by cooling, and re-collecting liquid.
Diuretic: increases urine and excretion.
Emmenagogue: promotes and regularizes menstrual flow.
Expectorant: removes excess mucous from bronchial tubes.
Filtration: process to filter out impurities.
Haemostatic: arrests bleeding/haemorrhage.
Homoeostasis: physiological process by which the systems of the body are maintained naturally at equilibrium.
Hypertension: high blood pressure.

Laxative: aids bowel evacuation.
Leucorrhoea: whitish or yellowish vaginal discharge.
Mucilage: thick aqueous solution used as a lubricant.
Nervine: reduces nervous disorders.
Oedema: excessive accumulation of fluid in the body.
Pathogen: any agent that causes disease, for example bacteria.
Purgative: aids bowel evacuation.
Sepsis: putrefactive destruction of tissues by disease-causing bacteria or their toxins.
Stasis: stagnation or cessation of flow.
Stimulant: increases one or more of the metabolic processes, such as blood circulation, perspiration, adrenalin secretion.
Stomachic: relieves gastric disorders. Tones stomach.
Sublimation: process of converting from solid state to vapour by heat and allowing to solidify again.
Sudorific: increases perspiration.
Tachycardia: increase in heart rate above normal.
Vulnerary: arrests bleeding in wounds and prevents tissue degeneration.

INDEX

acne 106
actions, therapeutic 36–46, 62–99
air humour 30–35
allergies 104, 107
aloe vera 62–3
ankles, swollen 109–10
antibiotics 119
antiseptic properties 42
anxiety 112
arthritis 110
ashwaghanda 96
asthma 102
astringent actions 41, 43–6
athlete's foot 107
Ayurvedic medicine 18, 27–35
constitutional types 31–5
elements 28–9
energy herbs 26
herbal qualities 29–30, 43–6
humours 30

back pain 110
barberry 85
basil 63
bayberry 63
blending herbs 60–1

blood-purifying actions 37–8, 43–6
blood-regulating actions 40, 43–6
boils 108
burdock 64
burns 108

calming function 21–3
carminative properties 36, 43–6
catnip 65
cayenne 65–6
chamomile 66
chickweed 67
chilblains 109
childbirth 116–17
children 31, 59
Chinese angelica 97–8
Chinese medicine 18
circulation 40, 61, 109–110
cleavers 67
clove 68
clover, red 87
colds 60–1, 103
colic 100
colitis 101–2
coltsfoot 68
comfrey 69

constipation 101
constitutional types 30–5
coughs 103–4
cramp bark 69
cramps 100, 115, 119
cumin 70
cystitis 105

dandelion 70
dandruff 107
dang gui *see* dong quai
decoctions 53–4, 58
demulcent actions 40–1, 43–6
depression 112
diaphoretic actions 38, 43-6
diarrhoea 101
digestion 36–7, 100–2
diuretic actions 39, 43–6, 61
dong quai 97
drying herbs 51–2

earache 103
echinacea 9, 60, 71
eczema 107–8
elderflower 60, 71, 71–2

INDEX

elderly 31, 60
eliminating function 21–3
emmenagogue actions 40
energetic qualities 25–6, 29–30, 43–6
expectorant actions 38–9, 43–6
eye inflammation 108

fainting 119
fatigue 113
female ailments 114–18
fennel 72
fevers 118–19
fire humour 30–35
first aid 119
flu 60, 103

garlic 60, 72–3
gathering herbs 47–50
ginger 73
ginseng 15, 26, 98
glands, swollen 109
golden seal 74–5
gotu kola 98

hawthorn 75
hay fever 104
headaches 112–13
heartburn 100

heat clearing actions 37–8
holly-leaved barberry 85
hops 76
hormonal changes 116
horsetail 76–7
hot flushes 115
humours 12, 18, 30–5, 43–6
hypoglycaemia 101
hyssop 77

indigestion 100
infections 108, 118–19, 119
infusions 53, 58
inhalations 54
insect bites 107
insect repellents 109
insomnia 113–14
irritable bowels 101–2

joint ailments 110–11
juniper 78

kelp 78–9
knees, swollen 109–10

laxative actions 37, 43–6, 61

lemon balm 79
licorice 79
life force 9, 26, 27
liniments 55
lymphatic ailments 109

male ailments 118
marigold 80–1
marshmallow 81
materia medica 62–99
meadowsweet 82
menopause 116, 117
menstruation 114–16
mints 82–3
mucous 31, 38–9
mullein 83–4
muscle ailments 110–11, 119

Native Americans 7, 16–17, 19, 47–8
nausea 102
nervous system 41, 43–6, 111–14
nettle 84

oak, white 94
oils and ointments 56–7

oregon grape 85

parsley 85–6
peppermint 82–3
period problems 40, 114–15
phlegm 31, 38–9
pine, white 94
plantain 86
poultices 56, 59
pre-menstrual tension 115–16
pregnancy 116–17
processing herbs 50–2
prostate swelling 118
puberty 116, 118

rashes 107
raspberry 87
red clover 87
reproductive ailments 114–18
respiratory ailments 102–5
rosemary 88

sage 88–9
St John's wort 91
sassafras 89
sciatica 111–12
sinus congestion 104–5
skin ailments 106–8
skullcap 89–90
slippery elm 90
sprains 111, 119
stomach problems 100, 119
storing herbs 52
strained muscles 111
stress 113, 118
styes 108
sudorific actions 38
sweet calamus 64
swollen glands 109
syrups 55

teas 53, 58
therapeutic actions 36–46, 62–99
thrush 117
thyme 92

tinctures 54–5, 59
tonifying actions 42, 43–6
turmeric 92–3

urinary system 39, 105–6

vaginal discharge 117–18
valerian 93
vomiting 102
vulnerary properties 42, 43–6

washes 54
water humour 30–35
water retention 105–6
white oak 94
white pine 94
white willow 95
wild yam 95
willow, white 95
wounds 42, 108, 119

yam, wild 95
yarrow 96